Table Of Contents

Foreword   7
    by Thomas G. Long

Preface   9

Proper 22   13
Pentecost 20
Ordinary Time 27
    The Joy Is The Journey
    Philippians 3:4b-14

Proper 23   21
Pentecost 21
Ordinary Time 28
    Recipe For Peace
    Philippians 4:1-9

Proper 24   29
Pentecost 22
Ordinary Time 29
    Somebody Up There Likes You
    1 Thessalonians 1:1-10

Proper 25   37
Pentecost 23
Ordinary Time 30
    To An Audience Of One
    1 Thessalonians 2:1-8

Proper 26   45
Pentecost 24
Ordinary Time 31
    Marks Of A Model Minister
    1 Thessalonians 2:9-13

Proper 27   53
Pentecost 25
Ordinary Time 32
    Arriving Home First
    1 Thessalonians 4:13-18

Proper 28   61
Pentecost 26
Ordinary Time 33
    Be Ready
    1 Thessalonians 5:1-11

All Saints' Sunday   67
    Becoming What We Are
    1 John 3:1-3

Thanksgiving   75
    Describing The Indescribable
    2 Corinthians 9:6-15

Christ The King   83
    A Prayer For Maturing Faith
    Ephesians 1:15-23

Lectionary Preaching After Pentecost   93

Foreword

In the Middle Ages, countless people traveled the long pilgrim road from France to the great shrine at Santiago de Compostela in northern Spain, where the bones of Saint James were reportedly interred. The pilgrim bands were a mixed lot — kings and paupers, the doubting and the devout, the sick hoping for a miracle and criminals under sentence, liars and saints, storytellers and minstrels, scholars and fools. Some went for prayer, some went for gold, some went as an act of penance, some went not knowing why, but all were beckoned by the great holy place at the end of the journey.

The road was hard and dangerous, patrolled by knights and plagued by robbers. Tiny villages and inns and churches sprung up along the pilgrim way to care for the needs of the travelers. One such place is Conques in the hill country of western France. It has been off the beaten track for centuries now, a place almost lost to memory. But, even today, the inhabitants of Conques have not forgotten they are a way station for pilgrims. They still speak the ancient tongue, langue d'oc, they still gather in their little church to pray for weary pilgrims, and they still offer comfort to the few who continue to travel the ancient road — tourists and hikers and cyclists.

Some years ago, an American, Hannah Green, was on vacation traveling the old pilgrim road with her husband, and the couple came upon Conques, where they were received by the residents with great hospitality. They soon fell in love with the beauty, friendliness, and faith of the village and decided to make Conques their second home. In her book *Little Saint*, Hannah describes going to the village church and hearing the pastor, Père André: "Something was there," she writes, "some force or power that could be felt ... I feel this immense and yet somehow humble, warming earth presence which is God filling the ancient church, swelling it somehow from silence into sound."

Gary Carver and Père André are brothers in the Spirit. Like André, Gary Carver preaches at a way station on an ancient pilgrim road, offering comfort and hope to the weary traveler. In Gary's case, the place is a Baptist church in the South and the pilgrim road is the pathway to faith that winds its way through the human heart. In these compelling sermons, Gary preaches to the mixed band of pilgrims jostling our way along toward the goal of spiritual discovery, and he speaks to our fears and doubts, our longings and our need, and most of all to our hunger to be closer to One whose presence forms the end of our restless trek.

As we hear his voice opening gifts from the biblical texts, telling powerful stories of human encounters with grace, encouraging us to keep trusting as we travel to that great holy place at the end of the journey, we, too, feel that "presence which is God filling the ancient church, swelling it somehow from silence into sound." Read these wonderful sermons and enjoy them. But, more important, read these sermons and take courage as you move faithfully along the pilgrim way.

> Thomas G. Long
> Bandy Professor of Preaching
> Candler School of Theology

Preface

These are ten sermons preached during the season of Pentecost without a manuscript before and with a congregation at worship.

Sometimes a preaching minister is overwhelmed with the inspiration of having something to say. Sometimes a preaching minister is overwhelmed by the responsibility of having to say something. These sermons fall into the category of the latter. They were hammered out on the anvil of having to answer the bell to preach each Lord's Day regardless of circumstance. They were forged from the background of 35 years of experience in the pastorate and fifteen years of service with this particular congregation, one that presents to the proclaimer the pressure of knowing good preaching whether they hear it from me or not.

Additional pressure was presented by the necessity of partnering these sermons with two complete different experiences of worship within the time expanse of three hours. A form of these sermons was given at a 9:15 a.m. service of contemporary worship within a time frame of ten to twelve minutes in the church fellowship hall where worshipers dress informally and singing is accompanied by a rock band. At 11:00 a.m. another form of these sermons was presented to a service of traditional worship in a time span of twenty to 25 minutes in a Gothic sanctuary accompanied by a majestic Aeolian-Skinner pipe organ. This challenge was not always easy or met with success. What is given here is a combined form and, I hope, a better effort of the two. But similar is the challenge presented every Sunday morning to many preaching ministers seeking to reach people for Christ in an ever-changing and consumer-oriented market. It is the most demanding and yet the most exciting day to be a proclaimer of the gospel of our Lord.

In these texts Paul challenges Christians, young and old, immature and seasoned, to live lives that are distinctively different

— lives that reflect the image of the risen Christ. He does this not by fuming and fussing or filling the air with ought and should. Paul does so by positing a positive image and challenging the churches to live up to it. He shies not away from placing himself as a model for them to follow or emulate. But he quickly presents the ultimate model for them to copy and that is the sacrificial example of Christ himself. Paul actually believes that we can share the very life of Christ and can grow every day to be more like him. So do I. That is definitely a life that is distinctively different.

As with my previous two books with CSS, *Out From The Ordinary* and *Acting On The Absurd*, there is no consistent style or form to these sermons. Each sermon draws its substance and form from its respective text as did both the contemporary and traditional services of worship. Again an effort was made to craft and present these sermons in a way as to preserve the oral nature of preaching. The worshiping congregation was invited to stand and hear the scriptural texts and the sermons were delivered without notes.

I want to express my deepest appreciation to the loving family of faith known as the First Baptist Church of Chattanooga. They not only help to make preaching a joy and worship an epiphany but had the boldness to begin a contemporary worship service in 1999, and the faith that their staff could meet such a challenge whether their confidence was misplaced or not.

I want to express my heartfelt thanks to the worship planning team at First Baptist: Mary Jayne Allen, John Echols, Jonathan Crutchfield, Nancy Bowman, Dave Smith, David Long, Karen Henderson, Melissa Phillips, Barry Kelley, Rodney Strong, Janice Bond, Harriet Grammer, Maria Stinnett, and Forebaye Guzenda. Our Tuesday morning and Sunday evening worship planning sessions are for me as much worship as anything that occurs on Sunday morning. These gifted people are responsible for the best that lies within the covers of this book. The technical expertise of Michael Jones, Brian Mays, and Chuck Wilson created an atmosphere every week into which the word sought to become the Word. The Connections Singers and Band are gracious to share their talents and dedication each Lord's Day.

Jo Ann Renegar not only has served as my secretary for ten years, but also has served as an accomplished editor, constant encourager, and cherished friend. Judy Sullivan, who became my secretary upon Jo Ann's retirement, applied polish and finishing touches which only improved this effort.

I am deeply grateful to my friend and mentor, Thomas G. Long, not only for writing the foreword, but also for sharing his friendship and mega-gifts with me and our congregation. A special note of gratitude is extended to Thomas Lentz and Teresa Rhoads of CSS Publishing Company for allowing me the joy of working with them on our third book together. Invaluable was their assistance.

Especially I want to thank my loving wife Sharlon who is the real strength behind anything positive I might accomplish. If there is such a thing as reincarnation, I would hope to come back as her second husband.

Lastly, I want to thank our parents and parents-in-law who have modeled to Sharlon and me as we grew up and to our sons, Chris, Brad, and Scott, as they grew up what it was to be distinctively different for Christ. I hope we have grown to be more like these four very special people to whom this book is dedicated.

Proper 22
Pentecost 20
Ordinary Time 27
Philippians 3:4b-14

The Joy Is The Journey

Sometimes, not every time, but sometimes the very worst thing that can happen to us is that we get to where we are going. This can be especially hazardous if the arrival to our destination does not begin another journey.

Many remember the popular television situation comedy *Different Strokes*. Recall the famous line, "What you talkin' bout, Willis?" Dana Plato, the young female lead, belongs to a long list of child television and movie stars who never moved beyond their early success. Recent news reports reminded us of her tragic death due in part to the fame and fortune at an early age that was not matched by continued success as her life progressed. Her career peaked early and possibly she saw the rest of her life as a downhill slide. Both of her male counterparts, Gary Coleman and Todd Bridges, also found early success but coped poorly when they were unable to continue at the top of the heap. Troubles with substance abuse and the law took the place of the acclaim of the crowd. Also add Bill Gray of *Father Knows Best* to the slate as well as Judy Garland. The list goes on and on.

The same dynamic can be applied to certain lottery winners who testified that instant money did not produce the guaranteed happiness that it had promised. In fact, I know of one family who won more than 500,000 dollars in a court settlement. In less than two years, not only were they broke, but they had also lost their home and had their new furniture repossessed.

The same dynamic also can be applied to those who have excelled professionally. One Nobel prize winner exclaimed, "It was the worst thing that happened to me! I didn't get any work done the whole year." The calling to ministry offers no exception. My own denomination is not the only one whose history is littered with stories of very gifted, charismatic, dynamic ministers who spent tons of energy and effort to reach the top only to find a shaky perch. Too many have fallen from grace and left shattered lives in their weary path.

Why is it? Where do you go after you "have arrived," especially at an early age? Is it too much, too soon, too easily? What does one do for an encore? And what about those for whom it was not a smooth or quick journey? What do you do when you finally arrive and have the job, salary, and spouse or live in the neighborhood you have always wanted? What do you do when the payoff does not supply the exhilaration and satisfaction you had expected? Does the ego drive that propelled such a rise have to find other worlds to conquer? Where do you go from the top? Can it be true that sometimes the worst thing that can happen is getting to where you are going?

Our text contains the personal testimony of one who arrived. He had it all! His name was Paul. Paul says, "I had it all," and surprisingly continues, "it was quite good!" Here Paul begins in verse 4 by publishing his pedigree. It is impressive! He does so in speaking against any unhealthy element in the church at Philippi who was preaching a false gospel of salvation by works. He calls them "dogs" in verse 2. Those probably were Judaizers, who said that one first had to be a Jew to be a Christian. These were probably legalists, stuck in a stage of growth, who exhorted forgiveness through rites and rituals rather than through grace.

Paul is stating that if anyone can be saved by works, he would top the list (vv. 4b-6). Paul was part of the best. He was a Jew — one of God's chosen people. The Jews were chosen of God to keep the traditions and the covenant made with Abraham. The Jews were chosen of God to record and preserve the Holy Scriptures. The Jews were chosen of God as the lineage through which God would bring his Messiah to bless the entire human race. They were the best! Paul says, "I am the best of the best. I am a Pharisee." There were no more dedicated and devoted students of God's laws than the Pharisees. Paul had studied under the very best teacher — Gamaliel! Impressive! Paul had a right to say, "If God's favor is based on merit, I deserve it all."

Implied in Paul's boasting is that his pedigree and position provided privilege. We, too, are not complete strangers to this kind of thinking. If we are not careful, we also can relate to others on the basis of their status, degrees, money, or family background. As I write this, I am aware that the current disappearance of John F. Kennedy, Jr., is made more tragic by the mere fact of who he is. Could it be true that Paul strikes out so vehemently against these legalistic preachers because he, too, had fished the stream from which they were spawned? He also once had been a legalist. He also once had been stuck in a stage of growth. Sometimes, not always, but sometimes we, too, most abhor the faults of others that we recognize in ourselves.

To his credit, Paul did not stay stuck. He saw a group called "Christians" who seemed to possess something he did not have. Was it because of Stephen? Although Paul's initial reaction was anger, he eventually, after being blinded, saw another opportunity to grow. The best of the best saw an opportunity to continue the journey. Paul saw that things could be better, even after "having arrived," especially if one was willing to change.

Is that how some child television and movie stars, like Ron Howard, were able to avoid the pitfall of Dana Plato and go on to find even greater success in another direction? Is that how Jodie Foster did not end up like Judy Garland? Is that what made Bruce Merrifield of Rockefeller University, after winning the Nobel prize for Chemistry, step on the elevator and go back to the laboratory where he had labored for 25 years? Is that what made a young millionaire attorney by the name of Millard Fuller give his money away and establish Habitat for Humanity? Is that what made Bruce Kennedy leave his job as president of Alaska Airlines at 450,000 dollars a year and become with his wife missionaries to China?

Is that what made Alexander Solzhenitsyn have a character in prison to say, "The happiness of incessant victory, happiness of fulfilled desire, always getting everything you want — that is suffering. This is spiritual death. It is not our level of prosperity that makes for happiness but the way we look at the world."[1] Could it be that Paul, after having arrived, saw in his world a chance to change?

When Paul saw an opportunity to continue the journey, he tossed away that which he had already gained. Fred Craddock states that verse 7 can be translated, "I tossed away everything." Notice that Paul did not devalue his past or what he had accomplished in his past. Paul "tossed away" something very precious to him and that to which he had given his life to attain. I had always assumed that before seeing Christ on the road to Damascus, Paul had come to the end of his tether, run out of answers, and was fully disgusted with life and his own spiritual condition. Craddock helped me to see that this was not necessarily the case at all. Paul had arrived! He was doing very well, thank you! But then, he saw something better. As good as he had it, he saw something even better. He saw something so much better that even a lifetime of lofty attainment seemed "as rubbish" in comparison (v. 8).

Notice that Paul did not negate his past. The man who had it all realized that his past was important and could continue to serve him well. When Winston Churchill visited the United States during World War II, he stated, "If the present quarrels with the past, there can be no future." Stephen Olford reminds us that the Roman god Janus (from which we get our word January) was depicted as a man with two faces. One face looked back into the year that had passed and that face bore traces of sorrow, dismay, and perplexity; the other, forward looking, personified hope and confidence.[2] Paul chose not to negate, to quarrel with, or to look back upon his past with dismay and sorrow. Paul chose to evaluate his past! Rather than getting stuck in the same mindless repetition of the past like the legalists he was speaking against, Paul chose to see the past as a stepping stone into a better future.

Keith Miller tells of attending a small group session where Alice told her story. "When I was a tiny girl, I was put in an orphanage. I was not pretty at all, and no one wanted me. But I can recall longing to be adopted and loved by a family as far back as I can remember. I thought about it day and night. But everything I did seemed to go wrong. I tried too hard to please everybody who came to look me over and all I did was drive people away. Then one day the head of the orphanage told me a family was going to come and take me home with them. I was so excited, I jumped up and down and cried. The matron reminded me that I was on trial and that it might not be a permanent arrangement. But I just knew it would be. So I went with this family and started to school in their town — a very happy little girl. And life began to open up for me, just a little."

"But one day, a few months later, I skipped home from school and ran in the front door of the big old house we lived in. No one was home, but there in the middle of the front hall was my battered old suitcase with my little coat thrown over it. As I stood there and looked at that suitcase, it slowly dawned on me what it meant ... they didn't want me. And I hadn't even suspected."

Alice stopped speaking a moment, but Miller didn't notice. He and the rest of the group were standing in that front hall with the high ceiling, looking at the battered suitcase and trying not to cry. Then Alice cleared her throat and said almost matter-of-factly, "That happened to me seven times before I was thirteen years old."

Miller said that as he looked at this tall, forty-year-old, gray-haired woman, he wept. She looked up, surprised and touched that her story had elicited such a response. She held up her hand and shook her head slightly, in a gesture to stop them from feeling sorry for her. "Don't," she said with a genuinely happy smile, "I needed my past — it brought me to God."[3]

Paul realized that he, too, needed his past. I think he would agree with songwriter Kris Kristofferson when he wrote, "I have a great future in my past." Perhaps Paul realized that with God nothing is wasted. God can use all of our experiences, good and bad, to fashion us into what he wants us to be.

Paul not only realized that he needed his past, he realized that he needed time. Paul was aware, as we should be, of those who espouse instant maturity and spirituality (v. 12). We emit a nervous laugh at the sign before the store that read, "Antiques made while you wait!" It takes time for the process of change and growth. It takes time for the journey.

Stopping to evaluate his past, the old Apostle said, "I had it all and it was good. I tossed it away when I saw something better. Now I strive for the very best" (vv. 12-14).

I think it was H. Grady Davis who said that a sermon should be boiled down to one sentence — to narrow its focus. It is not difficult to see that upon which Paul was focused: "For the sake of Christ" (v. 7); "I want to know Christ" (v. 8); "be found in Christ" (v. 9); "I want to know Christ" (v. 10); "Become like Christ" (v. 10); "Be in heaven with Christ" (v. 14). Paul's whole existence was Christ! He was focused upon Christ!

Mark Twain stated that the only people who like change are "wet babies." Not so with Paul! He embraced change especially if it brought the opportunity to be like Christ. Paul's continued journey was toward Christlikeness. The prize Paul sought was to be like Christ and to live with him forever (vv. 10-11, 14). Paul set out to continue the journey of growth that extends through eternity. We never have all the answers. To think so is to become stuck in a legalistic stage of growth which only leads to atrophy and spiritual death. The joy is the journey — the pilgrimage of discipline and change that conditions us to appreciate fully the destination. The joy is being aware of the tremendous price paid for us to travel the way. Our joy is our gratitude to the One who gave his all to enable us to walk in his steps.

This journey of discipline and change is best characterized by a story told by John Claypool. It seems that an Italian peasant met a monk one day who lived in a monastery upon the hill that overlooked the village. She said to him breathlessly, "Father, I have always wondered what you men of God do up there in that place that is so close to God." The monk was wise and humble and replied softly, "What do we men of God do up there on that mountain? I'll tell you. We fall down and we get up. We fall down and we get up. We fall down and we get up."[4] We all belong to the "society of skinned knees." But we know that when we fall, Christ gives us the power to get up and to continue the journey with him at our side.

In 1967, I was privileged to hear Gert Behanna give her testimony to the Pastor's Conference of the Southern Baptist Convention in Miami, Florida. She chronicled her life as an alcoholic through failed marriages and the disappearance of a child. She, like Paul, met Christ late in life and possessed one of the most vibrant testimonies I have ever heard. When she concluded, 17,000 gave to her a standing ovation which seemed to last five minutes. She concluded with a paraphrase of the old slaves' prayer:

> *Lord, I ain't what I ought to be.*
> *Lord, I ain't even what I could be.*
> *But thank you, Lord, I ain't what I used to be.*

It's a joyful and sometimes bumpy road to Christlikeness.

---

1. Alexander Solzhenitsyn, *Cancer Ward* (New York: Grosset & Dullap, Bantam Books, 1969), p. 266.

2. Stephen F. Olford, *The Pulpit And The Christian Calendar* (Grand Rapids: Baker Book House, 1991), p. 17.

3. Keith Miller, *Habitation Of Dragons* (Waco: Word, 1970), p. 184.

4. John Claypool, "Pressing Toward the Mark," an unpublished sermon preached at Northminster Baptist Church, Jackson, Mississippi, May 24, 1981.

**Proper 23
Pentecost 21
Ordinary Time 28
Philippians 4:1-9**

Recipe For Peace

"There is no God!" blatantly he shouted. He would cross his arms and scream up into heaven, "If there is a God, let him strike me dead!" Then he would wait defiantly for that which he knew would not happen. Bob was the most crude, profane, and distasteful person I had ever met. I met him in my third summer in the Republic Steel Mill in Gadsden, Alabama, working to earn money to go back to college to study for the ministry. And, oh, when he found out I was a young preacher! "Preachers are all liars," he spouted. "They all are just after your money. I don't believe in an educated preacher," he spewed about three inches from my face. For a man who said he did not believe in God, he sure used his name a lot. But, if one could wade through all that venom and vengeance spurting from his foul mouth, one would find that he probably believed in God as much as anyone. He was just mad. Years before, he had been a church person. But then his little daughter, his only daughter, had burned to death in a fire. He needed to make peace with his God.

"How's Buddy?" That is all he said. I was not there, but Dennis Fondren who owned the barber shop swears that is all he said. "How's Buddy?" With that reference to his brother, the man said not a word, got up, and walked out of the barber shop without getting his hair cut. Several years earlier, he and his brother, both wealthy, had disagreed over something, probably relatively insignificant, when their mother died. Now, he would not speak to or even speak about his own sibling. The man needed to make peace with his brother.

She had a very good husband. I knew him well. She had a very good husband, but she told me once that he was only a paycheck. She had a very good husband, but often she would demean and belittle him in public. She had a very good husband, but she was not always faithful to him. She had a close call with death — long hospital stay. My prayer as her pastor was that this premature brush with the inevitable would bring her to her senses. It made her worse! And her very good husband left her. "I've lost two," she said, "him and the baby I gave up for adoption before I met him." Her guilt was ruining her life. She needed to make peace with herself.

Peace! How do you define peace? It is not an easy thing. The United Nations might define peace as the absence of hostility. The Old Testament word for peace, "shalom," can be defined as "wholeness." "Be whole — non-fragmented." Paul might define peace as the result of the loss of enmity caused by sin between ourselves and God. That which has been separated is now brought back together or reconciled. How do you define peace? There are probably as many definitions as there are people who are reading this. However you define peace, you know when you have it and you know when you don't.

Paul knew that the church at Philippi did not have peace. Two women, Euodia and Syntyche, were at odds with each other. Do not picture Paul as picking on women or having an unhealthy attitude toward women in the work of the church or at Philippi in particular. We know from 1 Corinthians 11:5 that women prayed and preached in Paul's churches. We know from Acts 16:40 that the church at Philippi was begun and often met in the home of a woman named Lydia. In fact, these two women, Euodia and Syntyche, have stood side by side with Paul in the work of the gospel. Paul is saying that these two important leaders at the church in Philippi should get their act together.

Don't be surprised or dismayed because there was conflict in the church. There are no perfect churches. The one I serve is not perfect simply due to the fact that I am a member. In fact, our firm belief in the biblical doctrine of the priesthood of every believer guarantees that we reserve the right to have interpretations and opinions that may differ. The old joke is all too true that wherever you have three Baptists, you will have four different opinions. You also may have heard the story of the man who was rescued from a deserted island after many years of isolation. "What did you do all those years?" the reporter asked. "Well, I hunted, fished, and built those three buildings." "What are those buildings for?" the reporter pursued. "One is my house and the other is my church," replied the rescued man. "What is the purpose of the third building?" The writer asked. "Oh, nothing!" the man replied. "Nothing!" the reporter asked. "Well, if you must know," the man replied, "that is the church I used to attend." It seems that conflict is our common plight.

We have something in common "in the Lord," and what we have in common is greater than anything we can ever have in difference. Thus, Paul urges the church to "stand firm in the Lord" (v. 1). So, Paul urges that these two be reminded that servant leaders should set aside personal preferences and differences for the benefit of the fellowship "in the Lord."

In addressing this situation, Paul is giving a recipe for peace within the church and its individual members. In these closing words, which almost defy development, to possibly his favorite church, Paul is cramming into this last minute list directives and imperatives around the things that make for peace. He may be implying that this undefined peace may be a by-product of doing something else. He may be saying that one will not find peace through a frontal attack. God's peace may be his gift to us, a serendipitous wayside sacrament joyfully discovered by doing what we already know to do.

Perhaps Paul is pontificating that the first ingredient in this recipe for peace is to choose to think rightly. Paul professes that we can "rejoice always" (v. 4). We have to remember that Paul is in prison. Philippians 2 reminds us that he does not know from one day to the next whether he will be alive or not. The dreaded knock on the cell door could sound at any moment. Even in these circumstances Paul could rejoice without reserve. Needless to say, this is a deep-seated internal joy not dependent upon outside circumstances.

A colleague tells of a friend who once showed to her a wish list. It was headed by the entry of a new Cadillac and included in descending order a new house, a new boat, jewelry, and so on. The last entry on the list was "peace of mind." If the friend has to wait on the attainment of her list to have peace of mind, she may have a long wait. She is similar to the six-year-old girl who was expressing extreme disappointment to her mother because she had to be one of the children around the manger scene in the church Christmas program. "I want to be an angel," she said. "They are the ones who sing the songs of rejoicing. I can't rejoice unless I'm an angel." Most of us will never be an angel in this life or ever have the chance to be. But, we should not let it be a condition for our rejoicing!

An additional ingredient under the heading of "think rightly" in Paul's recipe for peace is "don't worry — about anything" (v. 6). In fact, worry changes nothing but the worrier, often to the negative extent that our creative juices are strangled and life is robbed of its vitality. A. J. Cronin states that only eight percent of our worries are legitimate, and the great majority of our concerns never occur! Emerson said it best:

> *Some of your hurts you have cured.*
> *And the sharpest you still have survived,*
> *But what torment of grief you've endured*
> *From evils that never arrived.*
> (From "Needless Worry" by Ralph Waldo Emerson)

This was illustrated to me recently when I read the story of the minister's mother who was worried to death that she was going to die of cancer. For 42 years she worried and worried. And, sure enough, she died — of pneumonia! For 42 years she worried about the wrong thing!

From a positive viewpoint, worry is a distortion of our capacity to care. The irresponsible seldom worry. From a negative viewpoint, worry is a mild form of agnosticism. Since we feel God will not or cannot act, we feel we have to take matters in our own hands and play the destructive game of "what if?"

Paul is saying that God is near (v. 5). We can trust him! It is said that angels can fly because they take themselves so lightly. Possibly we ought to take ourselves more lightly, take God more seriously, and take our worries to the God of peace.

The third ingredient in Paul's recipe under the heading of "think rightly" is to fix our minds upon the higher and finer attributes of life (v. 8). Here Paul draws upon the Greek moralists of his day, possibly Stoics, and baptizes these terms into advice for the Christian congregation. Think about, dwell upon, steadily hold onto whatever is true, noble, right, pure, lovely, admirable, excellent, and praise worthy. Paul is directing them to expose their minds deliberately to the creative impact of the positive realities of the highest and best. Again Emerson is helpful when he said, "A man is what he thinks about all day long." The computer folks say, "Garbage in, garbage out!" Paul's first ingredient is intentionally to mix well the decisions to rejoice, not to worry, and to saturate our minds with the higher things regardless of outside influences or circumstances.

Billy Graham tells the story of an Eskimo fisherman who came to town every Saturday afternoon. He always brought with him his two dogs. One was white and the other was black. He had taught them to fight on command. Every Saturday afternoon in the town square the people would gather to watch these two dogs fight, and the fisherman would take bets. On one Saturday the black dog would win; another Saturday, the white dog would win — but the fisherman always won! His friends began to ask him how he was so successful. "It is simple," he said, "I starve one and feed the other. The one I feed always wins because he is stronger."[1]

It is our choice as to which side of our nature we feed.

Paul continues by stating that we not only have the power in Christ to choose to think rightly, we also have the ability to choose the right role models (v. 9a). It is true that we become like those we most admire. I have had dozens of role models in my family like my brother, father, and grandfathers. Sports figures like Lou Gehrig, Sandy Koufax, and David Robinson have inspired me. Fellow ministers like Kress Davis, Scott Bryant, and LeVan Parker have often caused me to envy their bountiful gifts but have challenged me, as well, to develop the few I have. I have often said, "I would like to be like them." But I do not think I have ever said, "Be like me!" I am afraid that my example would not support my exhortation. Not so with Paul! "Whatsoever you have learned or received or heard from me, or seen in me — put into practice" (v. 9a). Wow! That is confidence in the witness of one's life.

I recently read the story of a father and his young son who approached a well-known sports figure to ask for his autograph. He willingly obliged. As he was signing their program the father said, "I hope that my son will be just like you when he grows up." The sports person stopped and replied, "What's wrong with your son becoming like you?" Good question! Is there anything wrong with those around us becoming like we are, especially if we are striving to become like Jesus?

The third and I think most vital ingredient in Paul's recipe for peace is his advice "to pray — with thanksgiving — about everything" (v. 6). This is the heart of the matter. God is near! (v. 5). Trust him! Put your energy into developing your relationship to him in prayer, in the spirit of gratitude, in all circumstances, good and bad.

To pray is to look life squarely in the face and to choose to deal with it. Prayer is not escape or avoidance. Prayer is not retreating into an ivory tower and losing oneself in a fog of other worldliness. It is not the Buddhistic approach of indifference.

To be honest with you, my efforts to avoid the problems of life have not met with ringing success. In fact, I identify with the story told by Halford Luccock recorded in *The New York Times* in an article by A. B. C. Whipple. There was in Australia during the 1930s a scholar of world events who foresaw that a great war was sure to break out. He realized that Japan would be one of the belligerents. Accordingly, this twentieth century wise man studied the atlas in search of the perfect hiding place, the best possible island of escape from the storm about to break across the civilized world. By the employment of careful logic and the process of deduction, he finally selected the spot, an obscure, virtually uninhabited island, and in the summer of 1939 he went ashore there. The name of the island was Guadalcanal![2]

I also can identify with Joseph Gallaher's statement: "Our human choice is never between pain and no pain but rather between the pain of loving and the pain of not loving." Prayer is not the place we seek to escape the pain of living and loving but where we share the pain with our Partner in life. He is near. We can trust him. And as we do so, we can create an atmosphere in our own hearts and minds to receive his gift of peace as it finds its way to someone else. Then, the God of peace will stand sentry, garrison, and guard our hearts and minds in Christ Jesus (v. 7).

The kind of peace that the God of peace gives (v. 9b) is more than the absence of hostility, more than wholeness or removing the barrier to reconciliation. God's gift of his peace is the presence of love — his love in our hearts. That is the main thing that makes for peace and defines a life that is distinctively different.

John Claypool relates a scene from the movie *Stars In My Crown*. It seems that there was an old black man, a kind of Uncle Remus figure, who lived in a small Southern town and had befriended three generations of children there in innumerable ways. He owned a little farm where he continued to live by himself after his wife died. And it so happened that some precious metal was discovered in that area and great pressure developed to buy up his property and to begin mining the ore. The old black man had not lived in a money culture, and he could not understand this "boom town" mentality. All he wanted was to stay in his familiar surroundings until he died, and so he refused even to talk of selling out. This led to increasingly angry confrontations. The banker in town and other commercial interests who wanted that land began to resort to all kinds of terror tactics. They burned down his barn, shot through his house one night, and finally issued the ultimatum that if he did not agree to sell by sundown the next night, they were going to come and lynch him — Ku Klux Klan style. The preacher in the community got wind of this power play, and so he went out to confer with the old black man. Come sundown that evening, sure enough, here came the leading citizens of that community, dressed in their white hoods, ropes and all, ready to hang an innocent man if they did not get their way. The old black man came out on the porch, dressed in his Sunday best, with the preacher by his side. The preacher told the would-be executors that the old black man was ready to meet his fate, and had asked him to draw up his last will and testament, which he wanted read at this time. With that, the preacher began to read how the old black man was giving his property and all the things he had to the various individuals who were standing at that moment ready to kill him. He willed the farm to the banker who seemed so anxious to get his hands on it. He gave his rifle to another of the men there who had first learned to hunt with it. He gave his fishing pole to another. In fact, item by item the old black man responded to the individuals who were preparing to kill him with acts of generosity and affection. The impact was incredible. Seeing goodness offered in the face of such evil was more than even these greedy men could swallow, and one by one, in shame, they turned away until the lynching mob had evaporated all together. The old preacher's grandson had been watching this whole drama at a distance, and after the crisis was passed and the two men had gone back into the house, the little boy came running up and asked breathlessly, "What kind of will was that, Grandaddy? What kind of will was that?" To which the preacher answered softly, "It was the will of God, son! It was the will of God."[3]

---

1. Billy Graham, *The Holy Spirit* (Waco: Word, 1978), p. 81.

2. Halford E. Luccock, *More Preaching Values In The Epistles Of Paul* (New York: Harper and Brothers, 1961), p. 208.

3. John R. Claypool, "Responding Creatively To Evil," an unpublished sermon preached at Northminster Baptist Church, Jackson, Mississippi, March 18, 1979.

**Proper 24
Pentecost 22
Ordinary Time 29
1 Thessalonians 1:1-10**

Somebody Up There Likes You

We are talking about encouragement. Carl Joseph was an exceptional athlete for his Florida high school. In fact, he earned thirteen varsity letters in football, basketball, and track. He stands six feet tall, weighs 180 pounds, and can jump six feet high, stuff a basketball, and throw the shot-put. Not bad for a young man with only one leg. Carl attributes his phenomenal success to the encouragement of his mother. She told him early in his life that the biggest handicap he would face was other people telling him what he could not do. His mother encouraged him to listen to the inner voice within that challenged him to be all he could be.

We are talking about encouragement. Nat came home from work, thoroughly discouraged, fired from his job at the custom house. Most distressing was his task of telling his wife Sophia. Her reaction took him by complete surprise. With an exclamation of joy, she said, "Now you can write your book." "Sure," he said, "and what will we live on while I'm writing it?" To his amazement, she opened a drawer and pulled out a substantial sum of money. "Where on earth did you get that?" he exclaimed. "I have always known you were a man of genius," she told him. "I knew that someday you would write a masterpiece. So every week, out of the money you gave me for housekeeping, I saved a little bit. So here is enough to last us for a whole year." So, Nat wrote his novel. Nat — Nathaniel Hawthorne who wrote *The Scarlet Letter*.[1]

We are talking about encouragement. William Bausch, the creative teller of tales, relates what seemingly was an autobiographical story in his early development. "In the first grade, Miss Grant said that my purple tepee wasn't realistic enough, that purple was no color at all for a tent, that purple was the color of people when they died and that my drawing was not good enough to hang with the others. I walked back to my seat, head bowed. With a black crayon, I brought nightfall to my purple tent in the middle of the afternoon."

In second grade, Mrs. Abate said, "Draw anything." She didn't care what. I left my paper blank and when she came around to my desk, my heart beat like a tom-tom. She touched my head with her small hand and in a soft voice said, "The snowfall. How clean and white and beautiful."[2]

How easily events could have gone the other way. Carl could have sat home with one leg folded under him in self pity. Nat could have gone from job to job for which he was ill-fitted and a masterpiece would never have been. A second grader may have heard another squelching voice of discouragement on a life-long journey and been sent off with unfulfilled potential.

We are talking about encouragement. But what happens when that word of encouragement is delayed? Dante Gabriel Rossetti, the famous nineteenth-century poet and artist, was once approached by an elderly man. The old fellow had some sketches and drawings that he wanted Rossetti to look at and tell him if they were any good, or if they at least showed potential talent. Rossetti looked them over carefully. After the first few, he knew that they were worthless, showing not the least sign of artistic talent. But Rossetti was a kind man, and he told the elderly man as gently as possible that the pictures were without much value and showed little talent. He was sorry, but he could not lie to the man.

The visitor was disappointed, but seemed to expect Rossetti's judgment. He then apologized for taking up Rossetti's time, but would he just look at a few more drawings — these done by a young art student? Rossetti looked over the second batch of sketches and immediately became enthusiastic over the talent they revealed. "These," he said, "oh, these are good. This young student has great talent. He should be given every help and encouragement in his career as an artist. He has a great future if he will work hard and stick to it." Rossetti could see that the old fellow was deeply moved.

"Who is this fine young artist?" he asked. "Your son?" "No," said the old man sadly. "It was me forty years ago. If only I had heard your praise then! For you see, I got discouraged and gave up too soon."[3]

We are talking about encouragement. But what if affirmation is delayed or does not arrive at all? In 1893 a young man enrolled at the theological seminary at Tiflis. For five years, he studied to prepare himself for the ministry until he was expelled by the seminary for reading a book thought to be inappropriate. The young man then turned his brilliant mind and boundless energy in another direction — politics. He, more than any one single person, was responsible for the imprisonment and murder of more than 20,000,000 people. His name was Josef Stalin. The benefits of encouragement can be astounding. The lack thereof can be tragic. But the worst case scenario is discouragement.

When encouragement fails to arrive and discouragement does, then enter the basement people. In Joyce Landorf's book *Balcony People*, she talks about "balcony and basement people." Envision the mind as housed in a clear glass or circle. The bottom two-thirds is filled with the dark, murky waters of our unconscious minds. The top third is filled with the pure, clear oxygen of our conscious minds.[4] Lurking in the dark murky waters of our unconscious mind is family or friends, living or dead, who continually reach up through that black water, grab us, and pull us under. Freudian psychologists call these people "basement people."

"Basement people" are the nay-sayers. They are the pessimists who have said, "You can't do this or that," or "You'll never amount to anything." These are the "sticky" people. They always are running others down by their snide remarks and innuendos. We are around them about five minutes and they have "stuck" to us all over, causing us to feel the need for a bath. These are the ones who invite us over each day for a piping hot cup of despair. They squelch any good word and often play the game of "ain't it awful!" These are those who emerge from the murky waters and remind us of the worst in ourselves and can drown us in negativism. They are the "basement people."

I have had more than my share of "basement people" some of whom did not even intend to be so. One said, "Preacher, every sermon you preach is better than the next one!" Another said, "That sermon was like water to a drowning man." Or what about the other who said, "Everything you said, preacher, applies to someone I know."

Sometimes I feel like the minister who was visiting Westminster Abbey in London and was told, "England's great sleep within these walls." He thought out loud more than he intended when he said, "Same as my church back home." One of the early kings of England was named Ethelred the Unready. I think I have served as pastor to some of his relatives. We all have had our "basement people." Even Martin Luther described his own spiritual journey as like a drunken peasant who struggled to get onto a donkey only to slide off on the other side. Such can be the effects of the "basement people" upon our lives.

Paul certainly had his "basement people" in Thessalonica. About 50 C.E., Paul and his teammates, Silas and Timothy, arrived at this metropolitan trade center and capital of Macedonia. Thessalonica had a Jewish synagogue and a center for emperor worship. The city was famous for its two mystery fertility cults, honoring Dionysus and Orpheus, which were known for their sexual and ecstatic indulgences (v. 9). In Acts 16:17-18, Luke tells the story of the beginning of the church. As was his habit, Paul first went to the synagogue and taught there, and people turned to faith in Jesus. His success was met with severe opposition, and the three men fled for their lives at midnight after only a few weeks.

From Thessalonica he went to Berea and the opposition party followed. They caused such a stir there that Paul had to leave. He then went on to Athens and later to Corinth. Silas and Timothy stayed at Berea. Apparent failure in Thessalonica, failure in Berea, and, some say, failure in Athens. In Corinth Silas and Timothy joined Paul and gave to him a positive report of all the good things that were happening in Thessalonica. Paul was encouraged by their report and wrote 1 Thessalonians to encourage and confirm the faith of the young Christians. This letter is the first New Testament book written as we know it.

Paul is encouraged by the work, labor, and endurance of the Thessalonians. They had not only received the missionary team but imitated them as well, to the point of becoming a model for the other churches in Asia. Everyone was talking about how they had turned from idols and turned to faith in Christ. They were the second church in Asia but first in example. How was the young struggling church able to overcome the loss of their founding pastor, a heathen culture, and severe persecution? In verses 6 and 7, Paul reiterates that they had followed his example and must now become an example to others. It was the law of the echo, what you send out returns to you. Paul was their encourager, and they in turn became his. The ill effects of negative, pessimistic "basement people" were overcome by encouragement. If we wish to break the destructive cycle of negative defeatism, we must become "balcony people."

Joyce Landorf goes on to talk about the "balcony people." These are the ones who live in the top one-third of our conscious minds, in the sphere of clear air wherein is the clean and pure oxygen. These are the ones who are not merely sitting there but practically hanging over the rail, cheering us on. These are our spiritual cheerleaders who continually shout, "You can do it! I believe in you! Persevere! Hang in there!"

Doesn't your mind explode with mental images of those in your past who have been your encouragers? I remember Mrs. Stone who won me to Christ. I remember words from my parents, grandparents, in-laws, and family that have sustained me. Pastors like Sidney Argo, teachers like Swan Haworth, friends like Harry Eades; the list is endless!

Some spoke the truth in love. I overheard my twelfth grade English teacher say to someone, "There is no telling what Gary Carver could do if he were not so lazy." She spoke the truth in love, she was a "balcony person."

Think of your past! Who are your encouragers? Who are your "balcony people"? Some of you may need to make a telephone call or write a letter of gratitude to those who have encouraged you. Quote to them Philippians 1:3, "Every time I think of you, I thank my God." You have had those spiritual cheerleaders, haven't you? Aren't you grateful that they have been there, applauding your success, forgiving your failures, and giving you another chance? A young preacher was so frightened at the delivery of his first sermon that he prepared three other sermons, just in case. He preached all four sermons in seven minutes. But he was encouraged by those around him. His name is Billy Graham.

Think of today. There are some right now, hanging over the rail, cheering you on. The Apostle Paul is there. The head cheerleader, of course, is our Lord himself, encouraging you. "Go for it! You can do it in my power, will, and love." Somebody up there likes you!

But let us take our thinking a step further. Are there not people in your sphere of influence to whom you can be an encourager, a "balcony person"? Isn't there someone to whom you can intentionally go to give what has been given to you?

Albert Schweitzer was once asked, "Why did you leave your status as a world renowned musician and world renowned theologian to go as a missionary to Africa?" His response was classic. He said, "It was about time I started returning something to the stream that had nourished me so." Is it about time we stop parking on someone else's dime and start feeding the meter ourselves? Is it time for us to start leaving time on the meter for someone else? Is it time for us to start being an encourager, a spiritual cheerleader, for someone else? You can be. You can start today.

It is our choice. We can be a "basement person," wallowing around in pessimism, griping, and grumbling, pulling ourselves down and everyone around us. Or, we can be a "balcony person," who encourages others only to receive serendipitously that which we have been giving to others.

For most of my 34 years in the ministry I have had people ask me, "Are you any relation to that old Preacher Carver who used to preach around Arab, Alabama?" "Yes, I am proud to say that he was my grandfather." My response then would bring the litany of stories about how my grandfather had touched their lives through encouragement. Roland Clemons approached me at a State Convention meeting. "I was picking cotton," he said, "with your grandparents. I turned to the old man and said, 'Preacher Frank, I think that God is calling me into the ministry.' " "Are you sure?" my grandfather asked. "I think so," Clemons responded. "Well, son, put down that pick sack right now and get to it!" "I lived with them for months," he said. "That old man would sit up most all night talking Bible and then plow all the next day. He was my early theological training. He was my seminary before I went to seminary."

In 1964, on the day before I entered college, we buried my grandfather. In the church he built with his own hands, his funeral service was conducted by six ministers, all of whom he had helped to start in the ministry. Seven if you include his son. Eight if you include me. I still have in my office the last postcard he wrote to me. In shaky script the concluding words were, "I have prayed that it be God's will for me to hear you preach God's Word." He died within two weeks. I entered the ministry thirteen months later. God did not answer his prayer. Grandpa has never heard me preach, or has he?

---

1. Jack Canfield and Mark Victor Hansen, *Chicken Soup For The Soul* (Deerfield Beach, Florida: Health Communications, 1993), p. 213.

2. William J. Bausch, *A World Of Stories* (Mystic, Connecticut: Twenty-Third Publications, 1998), p. 331.

3. Bausch, *op. cit.*, p. 301.

4. Joyce Landorf, *Balcony People* (Waco: Word, 1984), p. 33.

**Proper 25
Pentecost 23
Ordinary Time 30
1 Thessalonians 2:1-8**

To An Audience Of One

I sometimes sit in the sanctuary of the First Baptist Church of Chattanooga, recalling its distinguished list of ministers, and say to myself, "What are you doing here? You don't measure up. You cannot live up to their standards of excellence in ministry." And it is true. I can't even live up to my own expectations and standards, much less to theirs. I identify with a recent statement made about Henri Nouwen, the gifted writer of many formative books on spirituality. It was said that he spent his energy and effort to write about a life he desired to live but could not. I say to myself, "I've read Henri Nouwen and, Carver, you are no Henri Nouwen."

I also have difficulty identifying with Paul in the apologetic letter to Thessalonica when he states that he is a minister "approved of God" (v. 4), elaborating on his string of successes there. I identify with him when elsewhere he states that he is the "chief of sinners" (1 Timothy 1:15). I identify with him when he moans in the book of Romans that when he desires to do good he cannot and when he desires to refrain from evil, he cannot (Romans 7:18-20). I resemble those remarks!

But to identify with the ideals and standards in our text is a thing I find most difficult. Listen to Paul's recital in 1 Thessalonians 2:1-8. There was no residue of his being persecuted and driven out of Philippi. Instead, when he arrived at Thessalonica, there were no impure motives, no error or uncleanness, no guile or selfishness, no attempt to use flattery to conceal greed. Instead, Paul was courageous, gentle as a mother's love, self-giving, and sacrificial. No wonder the mission was a rousing success (v. 1)! Here is a minster who is seeking to please only God (v. 6)! Wow! I know that this is the way I am supposed to live my life and conduct my ministry, but there is such a great distance between the sky of my ambitions and the reality of my performance. I cannot duplicate Paul's example. I cannot even live up to my own expectations of myself. And what about God's expectations? How can I ever expect to please God, much less live up to my own expectation, whether realistic or not. How can you fulfill your own calling and please God? In short, who are we trying to please? Are we trying to please people?

Keith Miller introduced to me years ago the question, "Who is your audience? To whom are you playing your life?" He said that in a sense life is like a stage and we are like actors playing our lives to an audience for their approval and applause. We can give to our audience God-like powers of approval or disapproval. In fact, we can become "approval-holics" addicted to their stamp of endorsement. Our audience can be a person, a spouse, a mentor, or a parent — living or dead. Kenny Stabler, Super Bowl winning quarterback for the Oakland Raiders, once commented on playing for Coach Bear Bryant at the University of Alabama. "I would have done anything," he said. "I wanted so desperately to please that man!"

Our audience can be a group of persons. "They!" You know, "they!" "What will *they* think!" What will *they* think of me — *they* at the club, or the church, or the neighborhood? In covering high school sports for three newspapers I heard the account of a very gifted football player who kicked a 47-yard field goal in the State All-Star Game. Someone who knew the young man quipped, "If there had been 10,000 more fans in the stands, he would have kicked a 57-yard field goal." The question remains, who is your audience? Who are you trying to please? Who supplies your sanction?

Probably the best or worst example in scripture is Saul, the first king of the Hebrews. This tall, handsome, strapping boy was chosen to be king of Israel by God — by God himself! But it was not enough for him to hear God name him king, he had to hear it from the people as well. In 1 Samuel 13, Saul is waiting at Gilgal for Samuel to make the sacrifice before he enters into battle with the Philistines. Samuel is seven days late. The people are leaving. So, Saul, with blood on his hands, offers up the burnt offering. "The people were leaving," was Saul's comment to Samuel when asked why he had acted so foolishly. Later in 1 Samuel 14, Saul binds his people under an oath to fast as preparation for battle. Jonathan, his son, heard not the edict and ate honey. As horrible as it seems by our standards, Jonathan was to be put to death for breaking the oath. But the people said, "Not Jonathan!" And he was spared. That's what the people said. In 1 Samuel 15, Saul was commanded of God to destroy the Amalekites and all their possessions. After the victory, Saul set out to fulfill God's command when the people said, "These sheep and cattle are fine and fat. Let's keep them for ourselves!" That's what the people said! That's what Saul did. Because of Saul's disobedience, God rejected him as king of Israel. His prayers went unanswered. His successor was chosen and he sank into depression. In 1 Samuel 28, Saul, deeper still into despair, disguises himself and sneaks into the tent of the witch at Endor despite his own decree that such should be put to death. Sinking as low as one can go, he summons Samuel back from the dead and pleads, "Tell me what to do!" Saul asked the people what to do. Saul asked Samuel. He did not ask God until it was too late. Who was Saul's audience?

Saul depended upon others for a validation of his own worth and works not because he loved or respected them. Rather, he tried to use or manipulate others to buttress his own weak self-image. You may have heard the story about the preacher who stopped by his church one afternoon while the building was in the process of being redecorated. As he wandered through the building, darkness came before he realized. All of a sudden he found himself in a room with which he was unfamiliar. The door shut behind him. He tried the door to find no doorknob on the inside. It was dark and he began to panic. No one was around — no staff, no builders, no custodian! He waited for a moment so that his eyes could adjust to the darkness. Suddenly he turned and saw the figure of another man. He was frightened, but he regained his composure and said, "What are you doing here?" The man did not respond. He thought the man looked like him, only bigger, meaner looking, and ugly.

He asked again, "What are you doing here?" Again the figure of the man did not respond.

Just as he was about to strike out against the ugly man, his eyes better adjusted to the darkness and he found himself facing a mirror! Possibly it is true that when our own self-image is distorted, we panic and tend to strike out against others around us.

It also may be true that a warped self-perception will blur our own sense of what is important and what is not. Evelyn Underhill in her classic work, *The Spiritual Life*, states:

> *Any spiritual view which focuses attention on ourselves, and puts the human creature with its small ideas and adventures in the center foreground, is dangerous till we recognize its absurdity....*
>
> *We mostly spend our lives conjugating three verbs: to want, to have, and to do. Craving, clutching, and fussing, on the material, political, social, emotional, intellectual — even on the religious — plane, we are kept in perpetual unrest.*[1]

Some of the most miserable people I know spend every waking moment in mortal fear worrying about what "they" may think. They try to mask this fear with desire, "We want, I want"; or with boasting, "We have, I have"; or with the attention getting, "I do, I've been...." Often it is no more than an outward facade posted to shield an empty or noisy heart — a heart that God already knows. While we all wish to be respected by our peers, we can expend all our effort and energy in the exercise to have, to want, or to do, forgetting they have no ultimate significance and still leave unsatisfied the need "to be"! Joy in life is found as we become more and more who and what God created us to be. There is an old rabbinic saying, "In this life we sometimes have to choose between pleasing God and pleasing people. And in the long run, it is better to please God for God is more apt to remember."

Another reason to neglect the need for attainment and accumulation and the pursuit of the need "to be" is that things aren't always what they seem. Dudley Rose was the Merrill Fellowship advisor at Harvard. He told the story of a time he was called on the telephone by a bookstore clerk. "I have an old man in the store rummaging through some old books who says that you will verify his check. He is shabbily dressed and says his name is 'Mara' or 'Morrow' or something like that." Dudley responded, "Is this man tall, slender, and gray-headed?" "Yeah!" the clerk said. "Believe he is!" "Listen my friend," Rose continued, "if he offers you a check for the books, take it! If he offers you a check for the building, take it! Ever heard of Merrill-Lynch?" Things are not always the way they seem. And they are not with Charles Merrill either. Born to privilege, he spends much of his time and money seeking to eradicate illiteracy in the formerly Communist block countries. Why would he do that? Is he trying to please God? Maybe he feels God is more apt to remember.

How can we please God anyway? If we sometimes have to make a choice between pleasing God and people, how do we please God? I am not sure that I know, but perhaps it works somewhat with our heavenly parent as it does with our earthly ones. Are there not ways we can please our earthly parents? Does anything bring more joy to the heart of a parent than simply to talk to them? In spiritual terms we call that prayer. Are not our parents delighted and pleased when we go to see them and interact with them? In spiritual terms we call that worship. Do not our parents beam when they see us reflect the lessons they have taught to us? In spiritual terms we call that obedience. I personally think it brings great satisfaction to our parents when we reflect the name we received from them. I am a Christian. I truly believe that in some way the great heart of God is pleased when I feebly reflect the Name of the One by which I am called, the name of "Little Christ."

A grandfather spent his passion in his rose garden. It was a true joy of his life. His life was made more joyous as one day his three-year-old granddaughter picked a rose that already was his, gave it to him, and said, "I love you, Grandpa!" How much more is our loving heavenly Father pleased when we return our lives which already belong to him?

It is the wonderful lesson learned by Paul: "that we loved you so much that we shared not only the gospel with you but our very lives as well, because you are so dear to us" (v. 8). Paul is an example of the wonderful freedom we possess when we seek only to please Christ. It was the freedom espoused by Saint Francis when he felt he had to renounce the wealth of his family and the confines of the church in order to please God. It was not a freedom for irresponsibility or carelessness, but a freedom to be unhindered in one's love for God. It was the freedom from the necessity of having to please others whose preferences change as does the wind and the freedom to please the God who never changes. It is the freedom to decide before the opinion polls are in. It is the freedom to possess our possessions instead of being possessed by them. It is the freedom to give as God in joy gave to us.

God has not called any of us to please people. God has called us to love people and to serve people. We are called to please God. Don't you see how liberating that can be? I do not have to try to be like the great ministers before me or like Paul because I could not if I tried. That would be phony! All I have to do is to try authentically "to be" me. To paraphrase the rabbi: I don't think God will ask me when I stand before him, "Why were you not Billy Graham or the Apostle Paul?" I think he will say, "Why weren't you Gary?" If I can authentically try to be the best me I can be, that might be a good start in pleasing God and in playing my life to an audience of One.

Andy Tampling and his wife began their ministry in a small church in northern Florida. The first Sunday he was in the pulpit a white boutonniere appeared with his name on it. He put it on. Every Sunday the white boutonniere was there. Wearing a white boutonniere became his trademark. He had no idea who was sending it. He and his wife would often sit over a cup of coffee and imagine who in the church was doing that. They went to the florist and asked who was sending it. The florist said, "It's paid for in cash and they wish to remain anonymous."

As he moved from that church to the First Baptist Church of Opp, Alabama, the flower was there in the pulpit as before. "Well, whoever it is, they are sending it from Florida." They again would talk, "Well, could it be...?" Years later they moved to the First Baptist Church of Sylacauga, Alabama, and the flower was on the pulpit the first Sunday and every Sunday thereafter. They would discuss it. "Well, I think it is...." "No," she died. "It can't be her. It has to be someone else." He asked others. No one knew! The florist would not say a word. He then accepted a call to serve the First Baptist Church of Birmingham. The flower was sent anonymously every Sunday.

After seventeen years of pastoral ministry, Andy resigned to head up the Department of Retirement Centers for the State Convention. The second Sunday out of the pastorate, he was preaching a supply sermon in a church in Montgomery. As he and his wife were about to walk into the sanctuary, she turned to him and said, "This is difficult for you, isn't it?" He agreed, "Yes, it is." She said, "This is the first Sunday in seventeen years that you have not had a church." And then she said, "I'm sorry, that I forgot to order your flower."

With that he stopped cold still in his tracks. A lump emerged in his throat. He turned to her incredulously and said, "It was you? All these years, it was you?" He said that he wiped a tear with one hand and took hers in the other and walked into the sanctuary. Just a little flower!

There is no telling how long love can last if you don't care who gets the credit. It is called seeking to please the God who already knows.

---

1. Evelyn Underhill, *The Spiritual Life* (New York: Harper and Row), p. 24.

Proper 26
Pentecost 24
Ordinary Time 31
1 Thessalonians 2:9-13

Marks Of A Model Minister

Because he often banged his fists into people's faces, they called him Bam Bam. His name is Michael Godwin. At twenty years of age he was on death row at the state penitentiary in Columbia, South Carolina, convicted of rape and murder, a crime he denied, and already was considered by some to be the most dangerous criminal in the history of that state. The first time I read his story chronicled in Harold Morris' book, *Beyond the Barriers*, I cried. It is a tragic tale. Bam Bam never had a father. He was raped by the paper boy at age three. At five he set the family house on fire. At nine he entered his first reformatory and then was transferred to a mental hospital. His mother was married three times and one of his stepfathers raped Bam Bam. At fifteen he was arrested for stealing a car. At seventeen he was arrested for burglary. At twenty, this six-foot, red-headed mountain of muscle was on death row.

But there had been a chance, ever so slight. There had been a slim door of opportunity for Bam Bam when an adult male showed interest in and compassion for this struggling juvenile. He sought to move Bam Bam from his horrible home environment by inviting the lad to his house for the weekend. But the door of possibility was slammed shut when the man had sex with Bam Bam. That is when I cried; for the man who abused the boy was a minister. Because of this experience Bam Bam hated everything about the church and closed the possibility to God's influence in his life.

I cried because here was an individual who had ever so slim a chance to turn the tide and make a difference in someone's life and he tragically blew it! It is that same mixture of the emotions of heartache, sadness, anger, and disgust I have when a televangelist falls from grace. It is the same sickness I have when a colleague and fellow minister makes tragic mistakes, damaging the cause of Christ, wrecks his or her family, and litters the path with a trail of victims. I know that it could happen to me. No one is immune. I would not be surprised if I do not preach weekly to some who have been hurt by a minister who has betrayed his or her calling.

But let me quickly add, that is not always the case! For every lone wolf in shepherd's clothing, there are thousands upon thousands of ministers who have answered God's calling with faithfulness and unwavering commitment. For every one who eases into a tragic mistake, there are numerous servants of Christ who intentionally love Jesus with all their heart, love his people, and unselfishly go above and beyond the call. I know ministers who have more than ten years of schooling beyond high school to equip themselves to equip God's people. I know of missionaries who leave behind family and even children to satisfy God's claim on their life. I know of many bi-vocational ministers who toil at secular jobs only to give their "free" time to churches who might not have leadership otherwise.

In our text today we read of a bi-vocational minister who sincerely sought to be a shepherd of souls. In Paul we find many marks of a model minister, one who enriched the lives of his people and sought to serve as their spiritual father. He states: "For you know that we dealt with each of you as a father deals with his own children, encouraging, comforting, and urging you to live lives worthy of God who calls you into his kingdom and glory" (vv. 11-12).

One mark of this model minister is that even though separated from the church he founded, Paul hastened to keep the lines of communication open. We remember that Paul, Silvanus, and Timothy had worked to start the church in Thessalonica around 50 C.E., but were driven out by persecution (Acts 17). Paul, waiting in Athens, received an encouraging report from Timothy about the progress of the work since his departure. First Thessalonians is Paul's response to that report and his effort to keep the lines of communication open with his former congregation.

We also must remember that these are "baby" Christians. Young in the faith, they did not have a church building or the New Testament or a book on theology. All they had was their newfound faith, each other, and their spiritual father, Paul. He wrote to continue his guidance, to encourage and reconfirm their faith, and to assure them of his continued interest and prayers.

It is important for spiritual parents and biological parents to keep the communication going with their young. No matter how strained or loud it may be, it is best to talk. A scream is preferred to the death knell of silence, especially in this day of confusing role models and increasing family pressures. This was never more evident to me than after reading an April 12, 1995, *Newsweek* article on Bill Wyman, guitarist for the rock group, The Rolling Stones. Bill Wyman married a woman who was 34 years younger than he was. His son, Stephen, married a woman who was sixteen years older than he was. Now where it gets confusing is that Stephen's wife is Bill's wife's mother. (The father married the daughter and the son married the mother.) Stephen married his stepmother's mother. Bill married his daughter-in-law's daughter. Bill's wife married her mother's father-in-law and Stephen's wife married her daughter's stepson. What would really be interesting is if Bill and his wife have a baby boy. The boy's stepbrother will also be his grandfather and in all of this someone has to be their own grandpa. Confusing! In all the confusion of our changing family roles, it is imperative to keep the lines of communication open.

Max Lucado tells a story he heard from a Brazilian preacher in San Paulo. Maria and her daughter Christina lived comfortably in a poor neighborhood on the outskirts of a Brazilian village; modest furnishings, gray walls, dirt floor, but it was home. Maria's husband died when Christina was an infant. The young mother, stubbornly refusing opportunities to remarry, got a job and set out to raise her young daughter. Fifteen years later, the worst years were over. Though Maria's salary as a maid afforded few luxuries, it was reliable and it did provide food and clothes. And now Christina was old enough to get a job to help out.

Christina recoiled at the traditional idea of marrying young and raising a family. Not that she couldn't have had her pick of husbands. Her olive skin and brown eyes kept a steady stream of prospects at her door. She spoke often of going to the city. She dreamed of trading her dusty neighborhood for exciting avenues and city life. Just the thought of this horrified her mother. Maria was always quick to remind Christina of the harshness of the streets. "People don't know you there. Jobs are scarce and the life is cruel. And besides, if you went there, what would you do for a living?"

Maria knew exactly what Christina would do, or would have to do for a living. That's why her heart broke when she awoke one morning to find her daughter's bed empty. Maria knew immediately where he daughter had gone. She also knew immediately what she must do to find her. She quickly threw some clothes in a bag, gathered up all her money, and ran out of the house.

On her way to the bus stop she entered a drugstore to get one last thing. Pictures. She sat in the photograph booth, closed the curtain, and spent all she could on pictures of herself. With her purse full of small black-and-white photos, she boarded the next bus to Rio de Janeiro.

Maria knew Christina had no way of earning money. Knowing this, Maria began her search. Bars, hotels, nightclubs, any place with the reputation for street walkers or prostitutes. She went to them all. And at each place she left her picture — taped on a bathroom mirror, tacked to a hotel bulletin board, fastened to a corner phone booth. And on the back of each photo she wrote a note.

It wasn't too long before both the money and the pictures ran out, and Maria had to go home. The weary mother wept as the bus began its long journey back to her small village.

It was a few weeks later that young Christina descended the hotel stairs. Her young face was tired. Her brown eyes no longer danced with youth but spoke of pain and fear. Her laughter was broken. Her dream had become a nightmare. A thousand times over she had longed to trade these countless beds for her secure pallet. Yet the little village was, in too many ways, too far away.

As she reached the bottom of the stairs, her eyes noticed a familiar face. She looked again, and there on the lobby mirror was a small picture of her mother. Christina's eyes burned and her throat tightened as she walked across the room and removed the small photo. Written on the back was this compelling invitation. "Whatever you have done, whatever you have become, it doesn't matter. Please come home." And she did![1]

Paul not only realized the necessity of keeping the lines of communication open but also the wisdom of knowing when to be tough and when to be tender. Paul was tough on himself as he refused to take financial support but rather worked as a tentmaker so as not to be a burden on the young church (v. 9). Paul knew that he had the right to accept wages for his work and later on did accept financial gifts from the church at Philippi. But with this fledgling congregation he wanted nothing to hinder his witness. He wished that no one could accuse him of selfishness or self-promotion. Had they? Paul was there to exalt Christ, nothing less.

Paul understood concretely as does every good minister that a true servant has to give something of himself or herself. In 1973, I attended the retirement party of Raymond DeArmond who served the Berney Points Baptist Church in Birmingham, Alabama. He said something I will never forget. "I have never served a church that paid me what I was worth," he proclaimed. "If they had," he continued, "I would have quit." I think Raymond had a word of truth about the independence a minister must have from his or her congregation and the essential sacrifice to be made. If a minister is for hire, he or she needs to find another vocation. If a minister does only what one is paid to do, he or she needs to find another line of work. A minister must be willing to give of self, over and beyond what is required. That kind of self-sacrificial love is not for sale at any price.

Paul also could exert tough love and be demanding upon the church. In verse 12 he "exhorts and challenges" the young Christians to live lives worthy of God, lives that are distinctively different. The wording in the original language is strong. In Paul's mind, it was not an option! Toughness was a trait I observed in my father. He was not perfect. In fact, at times he could be very demanding. I never worked for a stricter boss. Equipped with the awareness that all parents bless and curse their children, he was the kind of father I try to be — prayerful that the blessings outweigh the curses.

When I was fifteen, I loved to drive our 1956 Chevrolet to the store, even though I did not have a driver's license. "Run down to the store and get a loaf of bread," my father said. "Sure, where are the car keys?" I replied. "Oh, you can walk," he answered. "No, I want to drive." "You don't have to drive." "I want to drive." "Fine," he said, "I'll go myself!" "What?" I said, not believing my ears. "I'll walk to the store myself." With that my father then proceeded to walk the two blocks to the Magic Market and back. I was standing in the yard when he left and standing in the yard when he returned. "I will not ask you to do anything, son, that I am not willing to do myself." I did not have to be asked twice again.

Paul, wise spiritual father he was, also knew when to be tender. In verse 12, Paul draws upon the image of the loving father who "comforts and encourages" his children. In verse 7, he uses the tender image of a mother who nurtures and comforts her child. In verse 12 he stresses the vital importance of constant encouragement to the development of the young Christians. Perhaps you have heard the story of the young girl who said to her dad, "Come play darts with me. I'll toss the darts toward the target. You stand there and say, 'Great!' "[2] Aren't you glad that you have had those spiritual encouragers in your life that enthusiastically said, "Great!" whether you hit the target or not?

Another mark of the model minister personified by Paul was his sacrificial example. No wonder the work flourished in Thessalonica! The young church had Paul as their personal example to emulate. In fact, the entire letter was a reconfirmation of their faith as to how they had put his words and example into action (v. 13).

Have you ever noticed someone who would behave a certain way or say a certain word and then bemoan, "Oh, no! I am becoming my father/mother." I know that I have. But in reality that is a wonderful endorsement of the parent. There is no greater compliment than to hear one's own words come through the lips of one's child. "My words have become the word of God in you," states Paul in verse 12. I think that was his intention. The word became the word because of Paul's example.

I was not surprised when first I heard the gospel. It did not surprise me to hear that there could have been someone so wonderful as

Jesus of Nazareth because I had seen someone like him in my father. It was not hard for me to believe that Jesus had risen from the dead because I saw him living in my dad.

When I was twelve years old, I pitched little league baseball. I was not very good, but my ineptitude was not due to a lack of encouragement from my father. The distance from the pitcher's mound and home plate was marked off in our driveway. Almost every day we would practice pitching. I would practice my only pitch, a fast ball and he would serve as my catcher. You ought to be aware that my father worked in the steel mill for over forty years. The constant exposure to the harsh detergents to remove the grease coupled with an inherited skin disease often caused the skin on his hand to break open. He always used a handkerchief in the glove to soften the blow of my errant throws. "Throw it as hard as you can," he would shout. "You can throw harder than that." I remember one day as we finished our practice he put his arm around me and said, "You had a good arm today. You really threw hard." He gave me his glove as he quickly put his white handkerchief in his pocket — the handkerchief that he had placed in his glove — the handkerchief with the fresh blood stains on it! An example! An imitation of Another who shed his blood that I might have an opportunity to become what I could be. I was not surprised when I heard the gospel. I was so blessed to have him as my biological and spiritual father. His example has made me a better minister.

Let me finish my story about Bam Bam. In March, 1982, Bam Bam was visited in prison by Harold Morris, an ex-con who was incarcerated for over ten years. It was a rough day. Bam Bam had beaten a guard and another inmate almost to death and was in solitary confinement. The night before he had attempted suicide. That did not deter Harold from talking to Bam Bam or from traveling the 500-mile trip from Atlanta to Columbia every week for years to do so. Slowly, agonizingly, but successfully, Harold led Michael Godwin to faith in Jesus Christ. Shortly thereafter, Michael completed a series of Bible courses and received his high school equivalency degree. He then was admitted to the University of South Carolina while still in prison. On August 16, 1986, Michael Godwin received his Bachelor of Arts Degree with a major in English and a minor in government. His grade point average was 3.85! Within a year, he received a Master's Degree from Luther Rice Seminary with a perfect 4.0 grade point average. His intention was to work on a Ph.D. Michael also received a new trial and a reduced sentence, but not the acquittal for which he hoped. All of this was paid for, arranged, and encouraged by Harold Morris through visits and over 500 long-distance phone calls. Michael has become a model prisoner influencing dozens and dozens for Christ. The orphanage in which he once stayed now buses their children just to talk to him. Bam Bam is surely a miracle.

Morris detailed a recent conversation with Michael. He asked him point blank, "Michael, you've spent sixteen of your 26 years in reformatories and prisons. You have a life sentence and could easily spend another twenty years in prison before you're eligible for parole. Today, would you trade your relationship with Jesus Christ for your freedom, so you could walk out of this prison?"

Michael didn't know the question was coming, but he never hesitated in his answer. "I would rather have the penalty of death and spend the rest of my life knowing I would die in the electric chair than give up my commitment to Jesus Christ," he said. "I love him with all my heart, and nothing in life has given me more joy than my personal relationship with the Lord."[3]

Did I tell you that Harold Morris, the ex-con, the spiritual father of Michael Godwin, the one who facilitated the miracle of Bam Bam — did I tell you that he is a minister?

There is still a good minister or two around.

---

1. Max Lucado, *No Wonder They Call Him Savior* (Multnomah Press, 1986), pp. 157-159.

2. Michael Duduit, *The Abingdon Preaching Annual, 1999* (Nashville: Abingdon, 1998), p. 348.

3. Harold Morris, *Beyond The Barriers* (Pomona: Focus on the Family, 1987), p. 118.

**Proper 27
Pentecost 25
Ordinary Time 32
1 Thessalonians 4:13-18**

Arriving Home First

His name is Ralph Archbold. Ralph Archbold delivers talks dressed in the character of Benjamin Franklin. He has been doing this for about twenty years in and around the Philadelphia area. Recently he spoke at an elementary school assembly program, and after the program he was invited to visit a fifth grade class that was studying American history.

As Archbold, dressed in the character of Benjamin Franklin, fielded questions, one of the students made the remark, "I thought you were dead." Ralph Archbold said, "Well, I did die on April 19, 1790, at the age of 84, but I didn't like that very much, and I just decided I am never going to do it again." A boy in the back of the class raised his hand and asked, "When you were in heaven, did you see my mother?" Archbold said, "My heart almost stopped. I wanted the floor to open up and swallow me. My only thought was, 'Don't blow this!' " Archbold said, "It was as though some divine word was given to me and I heard my voice saying, 'Well, I don't know if she was the one I think she was, but if she was, she was the most beautiful angel there.' " The boy's face beamed and that told me that I gave the right answer.[1]

The question has been phrased from the beginning of time. Millions have stood over freshly covered graves and wondered, "Where is my loved one?" But today no one wants to talk about death in our society. It has become taboo. We do our exercises, take our vitamins, dye or replace our hair, visit a plastic surgeon, and joke that we are going to be killed by a jealous husband at age 95 all in an effort to delay or deny the inevitable. But the undeniable truth is the mortality rate is still 100 percent. We are all terminal, and so are those we love. When they precede us in the journey, the question is all too agonizingly real: "Where is my loved one?" It is the question stated by the church at Thessalonica to the Apostle Paul that gives rise to our text.

Paul started the church in a whirlwind of persecution and in a sparsity of time. Having heard Paul's witness for only a few weeks, the theological vocabulary of the young fellowship was sketchy at best: Jesus lived, Jesus died, Jesus rose from the dead, Jesus is coming again, possibly very soon. Knowing only the barest of essentials and excited about Jesus' possible imminent return, they asked, "What about my Christian loved one who is already dead or one who dies prior to his coming? Does that person lose out on the promised deliverance of the Messiah?" The idea of a bodily resurrection had little background in a Gentile world probably dominated by the Greek notion of the immortality of the soul. While our context may have changed, the question remains the same. We join the millions of voices who have asked, "What has and will happen to my loved one?"

Our question has at least two possible perspectives. One possibility comes from the mouth of Job, that Old Testament figure, when he said, "Man born of woman is few of words, few of days, and full of troubles. He springs forth like a flower and then he withers." This is a life without God. This is a life without purpose, direction, and meaning. This is a life of despair and pessimism that quickly recedes into cynicism.

This cynicism is evident in a pagan epitaph from the first century. The epitaph read: "I was not, I became. I am not, I care not." This is a world without God. This is a world without hope that descends into despair and selfishness. Existence becomes an exercise centered around self. All one can acquire, accumulate, and amass becomes the placebo to soothe the hunger within us for something we know not what.

On August 17, 1995, the University of Connecticut raised the salary of the coach of the women's basketball team to $170,000 after the team won the National Championship. This was a $73,000 a year raise! At the same time they raised the men's basketball coach's salary from $300,000 to $335,000 a year. The president of the university made $135,000 a year, and the average professor made $74,000 a year. There was a time when the center of our universities was the chapel or the library or the classroom. Is it true that now it has become the athletic field? And how much do we pay Michael Jordan? When we pay those who entertain us more than we pay those who teach us, something is wrong with our priorities. It is a world based upon cynicism. It is a world based upon selfishness. It is a world without hope. It is a world in despair.

Pierre and Marie Curie were the greatest scientists of France since Louis Pasteur. Together they discovered radium. They won three Nobel Prizes. They had everything going in the world except a belief in God. In April of 1906, Pierre Curie absent-mindedly wandered into the street in front of a team of horses pulling a wagon. He was killed instantly. They should have buried Marie as well, because for her it was the end of life. She wrote in her diary: "Everything is over. They dug a grave and put sheaves of flowers over Pierre, and he sleeps his last sleep under the earth; but for me, everything is gone. Everything!"[2] "Man born of woman is few of words, few of days, and full of troubles. He springs forth like a flower and then he withers." It is a world of cynicism, selfishness, and despair. It is a world without God.

But Paul speaks of another possibility. We do not have to live lives of cynicism, selfishness, and hopelessness. We can live lives that are distinctively different. The joyful alternative is found in the words,

> *Brothers and sisters, we do not want you to be ignorant about those who fall asleep or to grieve like the rest of men who have no hope. We believe that Jesus died and rose again and so we believe that God will bring with Jesus those who have fallen asleep in him. According to the Lord's own word, we tell you that we who are still alive, who are left till the coming of the Lord, will certainly not precede those who have fallen asleep.* — 1 Thessalonians 4:13-15

No one will be left out! There will be no broken circle or empty chairs. All God's children will be with him forever. "Therefore, encourage each other with these words" (v. 18). Jesus has risen from the dead. He is alive and so shall we be.

It is easy to get so preoccupied with the timing, location, and procedure of the Second Coming that we forget the purpose of its message. The Good News proclaims that death is not an exit but an entrance. Our loved ones are in the sight of God. We all will be united with Christ. This word should cause us to take joy and delight in its warm assurance that is nothing less than miraculous.

Resurrection is a miracle. It is not our right. It is not our nature. Resurrection is a miracle! Resurrection is a gift from God. "For the wages of sin is death, but the gift of God is eternal life through Jesus Christ our Lord" (Romans 6:23). Resurrection is God's miracle; therein we greatly rejoice.

Let us be realistic. Many of us already have had a full life filled with far more than we ever deserved. But we, too, can rejoice in God's grace. We also can rejoice that God's grace is extended to others, especially to those who have not been so fortunate as we have been. Think about those who never had a chance. Is not the resurrection God's assurance that his grace will be extended to them? I think of the baby, born with AIDS, who dies quickly, never having any opportunity at life. Resurrection grace says, "I love you." I think of all those who are trapped in homes for the mentally ill. My first year in seminary, I worked at the Central State Hospital in Anchorage, Kentucky, where over 1,200 patients were housed. I saw children who never had one minute's chance. One family produced Jimmy and Darlene, both hopelessly mentally retarded and physically challenged from birth. Resurrection grace says, "There's another world!" I think of the families extinguished by the greed, poverty, and violence of war. Resurrection grace says, "One day we will make war no more." I think of the 20,000 children who die in our world every day from malnutrition. Resurrection grace says, "One day you will sit at the bounty of God's table." To all of those who never had a chance or had the bud of opportunity crushed before it was ever allowed to bloom, resurrection grace says, "There is another world coming with beginnings without end."

Because Christ is risen we can not only rejoice in his grace but also live our lives in a community of caring people. We call it the church. It is the place where we pray for each other, comfort each other, bear one another's burdens, and love each other through the crises of life, even the loss of a loved one. It is a "different" place.

A park ranger was once asked, "How do the giant sequoias live? How do they last so long with such a shallow root system?" The ranger replied, "The sequoias have learned to interlock their root system and interlock their branches so when the fierce winds come, they stand together." So when the fierce winds hit us as a community of faith we stand together. When we hear the death bell ring, we interlock and stand with each other.

A recent widow told me, "I knew this day would come. He was older and we married late. I always knew that he would precede me in death. But, instead of casting a dark cloud, our awareness of that enabled us to live each and every day to its fullest." Because Jesus lives, we can live in a community of caring people. We can live each and every day to its fullest and look toward the future with hope, encouragement, optimism, and faith.

It was said that Beethoven knew that the keyboards of his era were not perfected. So he wrote music that could only be played on instruments not yet built. We build our lives on a foundation that is solid and on a completion that is not yet. We live in the now as resurrected people and as a community of faith. Because Jesus lives, we shall live also, looking forward to the future when we shall be reunited with those who have gone on before us. We are to comfort one another with these words.

Joseph Schultz was a German soldier in World War II. Shortly after his indoctrination he was sent to Yugoslavia right after the invasion. One day his sergeant gathered eight soldiers, Schultz being one of them. After they had walked over two hills, they came upon eight Yugoslavian peasants, five women and three men. As they were told to line up, Schultz realized what his mission was. "Ready! Aim!" With that the silence was broken by the thud of a rifle butt as it hit the ground.

Joseph Schultz tossed his weapon aside, and began to walk toward the Yugoslavian peasants. The sergeant cried out, "Come back here!" The sergeant was ignored. Joseph Schultz walked the fifty feet to the peasants. As they were holding hands, he joined hands with them. The German sergeant cried, "Fire!" Joseph Schultz died and mingled his blood with that of the innocent peasants.

A note was found in Joseph Schultz's pocket from the writings of Saint Paul which said, "Love does not rejoice in evil, but love rejoices in the truth. Love always trusts. Love always hopes. Love always perseveres."[3] Joseph Schultz went to his death with no guarantee, with no assurance, with no hope other than the one you have today.

Fred Craddock tells the story of Anson Mount. After serving as the religion editor for a national magazine, Anson retired. He decided to retire to his boyhood home of White Bluff, Tennessee, just north of Nashville. He never gave his decision a second thought until he arrived at the small town. As he looked around, he asked himself, "What am I doing here? I have been away for 25 years. Does anyone here know or remember me?"

Contemplating his decision, Anson noted that his gas gauge was reading on "empty." So, still lost in thought, he pulled up to an old country store which had a gas pump in front. After several minutes, an old man emerged from the store, sorely took his time descending the steps and slowly ambled over to Anson's automobile. The old codger never said a word, stuck his head into the window of the car, and waited. Anson finally said, "Uh, fill 'er up!" The old man just nodded and took his easy time going to the back of the car. It seemingly took an eternity and a day to pump the petro. Moving at his own pace, the old man deliberately put up the hose, closed the flap, and came back around to where Anson was sitting. The old fellow finally broke his silence when he looked into the window and said flatly, "Anson, you want to pay for this now or you want to put this on a bill?"

And Anson knew he was home!

Jesus lived, Jesus died, Jesus rose again. Jesus is coming back. Our loved ones are with him. Our loved ones are at home!

1. Jack Canfield and Mark Victor Hansen, *A Second Helping Of Chicken Soup For The Soul* (Dearfield Beach, Florida: Health Communications, 1993), pp. 171-172.

2. Ralph M. Small, *Standard Lesson Commentary* 1972-1973 (Cincinnati: Standard Publishing, 1971), p. 363.

3. William J. Bausch, *Timely Homilies* (Mystic, Connecticut: Twenty-Third Publications, 1990), p. 55.

**Proper 28
Pentecost 26
Ordinary Time 33
1 Thessalonians 5:1-11**

Be Ready

I am sure that most of you shook the slats out of the cradle when you first heard the following story. But it is a good one and illustrates a point I would like to make. It seems that the young preacher pranced up to the pulpit prepared to preach his first sermon with no notes — no safety net. Prepared he was, he thought. As he looked over the congregation, his mind went into neutral, blank, *tabula rosa*! He could not think of a single thing! His confidence quickly turned to embarrassment. Sweat beads popped out on his forehead. He became desperate. The congregation stared at him with concern. Some began to elbow one another.

He was about to sit down when he remembered a scripture from the text, Revelation 22:7, where Jesus says, "Behold, I come quickly!" So, he struck the pulpit firmly and bellowed with renewed confidence, "Behold, I come quickly!" Nothing came! Still hopeful that the text would trigger additional memory, he tried it a second time. "Behold, I come quickly!" he shouted a little louder and pounded the pulpit more firmly. Still, nothing came! The perplexed congregation stared more intently.

Now panic stricken, he thought to himself, I am going to try this one more time. If nothing happens, I am never going to do this again. So, he took three or four steps backward and then ran to the pulpit, hit it as hard as he could, and shouted at the top of his voice, "Behold, I come quickly!" Sure enough, he did. He, pulpit, and all tumbled out into the congregation. The pulpit went one way and he landed in the front pew in the lap of a beautiful elderly lady, the picture of everyone's favorite grandmother. After being initially dazed, realizing what he had done, he began to apologize profusely, "I'm so sorry! I'm so sorry!" he said. "Oh, no, sonny, don't fret! It's all my fault. I should have moved. You told me three times you were coming!"

We are talking about the Second Coming of our Lord. He is coming again and some believe that he is coming quickly. Paul thought so as he wrote to the young church in response to their questions about the timing of the parousia. Paul says that our Lord will come suddenly like the labor pains upon a woman in travail beginning an irreversible process (v. 3). There will be no escape for anyone, no more than the woman can change her mind about whether to have the baby or not. Our Lord will also come unexpectedly like a thief in the night (v. 2). He will come when some are least aware. They will be caught off guard and unprepared. If his coming is so sudden and unexpected, how foolish of us to try to predict the time (Acts 1:7). If Jesus himself does not know, how could we? We must live in a constant state of readiness.

William Carter in his book, *No Box Seats In The Kingdom*, reports the Jehovah's Witnesses have changed their minds. After warning for decades that the world would end within this present generation, the leaders of the sect announced in December, 1995, that they have softened their position. Their reasoning is that Jesus' words in Mark 13 referred "to his generation and not ours."[1] The conclusion by an ex-Witness was that if they ceased to believe that Jesus was coming back tomorrow they would have more difficulty recruiting members today. It is difficult to be critical of the Jehovah's Witnesses because they probably have become more like most of us. We, too, have lost our sense of urgency. We reason that it has been 2,000 years and he still has not come. Could it be that we, too, have lost our sense of immediacy, and our enthusiasm for his coming has waned?

Fred Craddock states that the problem with preaching of a generation ago was that it was poorly prepared. He goes on to state that the problem with the preachers of today is they preach as if nothing is at stake. Have we lost our sense of urgency?

One's eternal destiny is at stake! The first time we hear the gospel can be either the best day or the worst day of our lives. It can be the best day in that we have the opportunity to say, "Yes," to God's invitation and to inherit all he has for every child of God: grace, forgiveness, a home in heaven. It can be the worst day in that we have the opportunity to say, "No," to God's invitation and will have to bear the responsibility for that negative decision.

It is also true with the Second Coming of our Lord or death, whichever comes first. To some it will be the most glorious day of their existence. It will be a day of long anticipated reunions, the beauty of heaven, and claiming our inheritance as a child of God and a joint heir of Jesus Christ. To some it will be the greatest day of all because we shall see Jesus, bow at his feet, and thank him for his love and unmeasurable grace. It will be a day when everything wrong is made right. But to others it will be the most tragic day of their existence. Everything wrong will be made worse, and they will bear eternal responsibility with weeping and regret.

Paul states that God has not appointed us to suffer wrath but to receive salvation through Jesus Christ our Lord (v. 9). It is time to be prepared. The University of Louisville Cardinal basketball team went to a tournament several years ago in Hawaii. At their first practice session in Maui, they discovered that the managers had forgotten to bring basketballs. They looked around in dismay and then heard a basketball bouncing outside the gym. They saw a young lad with an old battered, well worn basketball. They tried to buy the basketball from the young man. "Ten dollars?" "No!" "Fifteen dollars? Twenty-five dollars? Fifty dollars?" "No! I'll not sell my basketball." In the meantime one of the Cardinal players said to the little boy, "You know, fellow, you're dumb. You could have sold that basketball for fifty dollars." The little boy scratched his nose and said, "Well, mister, I may be dumb, but at least I'm smart enough to know that if you're going to practice basketball you need to bring a basketball!"[2]

Paul, in our text, tells us how we can be prepared for death or the Second Coming no matter when it may come. To keep us from dropping the ball, he states in verse 6 that there are some things we can intentionally and purposefully do. We can be watchful. We can be alert, aware, in a state of constant readiness. What does that mean? Be alert for "signs" of his coming? Be alert for the moving of his Spirit? Be alert for others? Do you know anyone that is unprepared? Have you said anything to them about it?

Recently the inhabitants of the Florida and Carolina coasts were bracing themselves for the possible onslaught of Hurricane Dennis. They were buying plywood, fuel oil, bottled water. Only a tiny fraction of those people ever needed those provisions. But they did not want to take a chance. Do you want to take a chance?

We must not only be alert, but also we must be self-controlled (v. 6). There is a phrase today which is getting common usage. When someone is about to get on the edge or say something they should not, someone might declare, "Don't go there!" "Don't go there!" If we are children of the light and day, then there are some places in darkness to which we should not go (v. 5). Don't go there. The preacher knew that he was on the wrong side of town. His excuse was that he was taking clothes to a needy family. He did not know that the woman was a cop. Solicitation was the charge. He lost his church. He lost his career. Don't go there!

She always liked to flirt. It was just harmless fun. Then she came on a little too strong and he came on a little too strong. Nothing really happened. But the friendship between two families was destroyed and the gnawing seeds of suspicion lingered for a long time. Don't go there!

Paul says that we are children of the light. We can be self-controlled. Or, better yet, we can be under Christ's control. The best avenue of preparation is to place Christ at the very center of our lives and to nurture our intimate and personal relationship to him each and every day. Be alert to his presence in our life. Don't go anywhere you would not want him to be with you. For he is, you know!

Paul states that we not only can be watchful, we also can be who we are (v. 8).

Beverly Roberts Gaventa in her commentary on 1 Thessalonians in the Interpretation Series, states that the syntax of the Greek indicates that we already wear the items of faith, love, and hope.[3] They already are ours because we are already his children. We wear them because he does. These are not so much actions we take as they are characteristics of who we are. We are faithful because we believe in the power of the gospel to change people's lives. We are hopeful of his triumphal return and of our home in heaven. We are loving because his love dwells in our hearts. Yes, we intentionally do certain things, be alert and self-controlled, but we do them out of what and who we are. We are not afraid or surprised (v. 4) because we are children of the light and faith, hope and love are God's gifts to us. We cannot merit or earn these characteristics. They are his grace gifts to us — the gifts of his very nature.

Charles H. Spurgeon once received from Andrew Bonar a copy of the latter's commentary on Leviticus. Spurgeon thought it to be excellent and returned it to Bonar with the request that the author autograph the copy and place a picture on the title page. Bonar obliged with the following note. "Dear Spurgeon, Here is the book with my autograph and my photograph. If you had been willing to wait a short season, you could have had a much better picture. When I see Christ, I shall be like him!" The more and more we prepare, the more and more we become who or what we are.

Some things we can do to prepare for his coming and they come from what we are. But we are what we are because of what he did. "He died for us so that, whether we are awake or asleep, we may live together with him" (v. 20). He died for us. Because of his sacrificial death, we do not have to be afraid. We can anticipate his coming with joyful enthusiasm. We can be encouraged and be encouraging, because of what he did.

Karl Barth said, "Precisely when we realize that we are sinners, do we perceive that we are brothers (and sisters)?"[4] When we truly understand that we are all sinners, we realize that we all are in the same boat. We need what only Christ can do. How thankful we are that he died for us. A. M. Hunter reminds us of a scene in Richard Jefferies' book, *Bevis, The Story Of A Boy*. The boy Bevis had a Bible with pictures in it, one depicting the crucifixion. The picture disturbed him very much. The cruel nails, the horrible mixture of sweat and blood, the pierced side, the marks and the lashes of the whip, the mockery of the crown of thorns, all threw him into anguish. After looking long upon the page, he cried, "If God had been there, he wouldn't have let them do it." "If God had been there...!"[5] Oh, but he was there! He was more there than he has ever been anywhere! He was there and he did let it happen — to show how much he loves you! He was there to show us how much it cost to save a world of sinners! "He that spareth not his own Son, but delivered him up for us all, how shall he not with him, freely give us all things?" (Romans 8:32).

The morning was not far spent when the weary pastor made her way across the hospital parking lot. The night had been long as she prayed with, comforted, and then tried to console a young couple as their small child left this world for the loving hands of its heavenly Father.

Her heart was heavy with things eternal when she almost bumped into a mother and her small daughter. "Please forgive me, I'm sorry," she said as she sought to be on her way. "I know you," the little girl declared. "Aren't you that preacher? Aren't you the preacher in that big red church?" "Why, yes, honey, I am," the pastor responded. "Tell me something, preacher," she said. "Where is heaven?" "I beg your pardon!" "Heaven, how far away is heaven?" the little girl asked. "Let's see, honey, place your hand over your chest and tell me what you feel?" "My heartbeat," she responded. "I feel my heartbeat!" "That's just how far away heaven is, honey," the pastor responded, "one single heartbeat!"

---

1. William G. Carter, *No Box Seats In The Kingdom* (Lima, Ohio: CSS Publishing Company, 1996), p. 61.

2. *Preaching*, Volume IV, No. L, July-August 1988 (Jacksonville: Preaching Resources, 1988), p. 34.

3. Beverly Roberts Gaventa, *Interpretation: First And Second Thessalonians* (Louisville: John Knox Press, 1998), p. 72.

4. Frank Stagg, *The Book Of Acts* (Nashville: Broadman Press, 1955), p. 70.

5. A. W. Hunter, *Preaching The New Testament* (Grand Rapids: William B. Eerdmans, 1963), p. 92.

All Saints' Sunday
1 John 3:1-3

Becoming What We Are

Shell-shocked soldiers presented a perplexing problem for the French Army following the conclusion of World War I. So shell-shocked were such soldiers, over 100 in number, that they had amnesia. They could not remember their own names. They were healthy in every other way, ready to return home to their families, but they could not remember their own identity. The French Army, due to a faulty record-keeping system, did not know who they were either. Perplexing problem!

It was suggested that the French Army hold an identification rally in an effort to name these homeless heros. After invitations to would-be families had been sent, interested parties were gathered in a large plaza in Paris. One by one these amnesia-ridden victims made their way to the microphone and pleaded, "Can anyone out there please tell me who I am? Can you please tell me my name?" Reporters gathered for the rally stated that few events in the entire war rivaled this one for its sheer drama.

What is your name? Who are you? Who are you now and who or what are you becoming? These are questions to which John is addressing himself in our text. John says that we are children of God. "How great is the love the Father has lavished on us, that we should be called children of God! And that is what we are!" (v. 1a). John paradoxically states that we both are and are becoming children of God.

Just think! We are children of God! How lucky! How blessed we are to be God's children! How blessed we are to be born into a world where God created everything "good." How blessed we are that God created us in his own image. How blessed we are that God himself breathed into our mouths the very breath of life. And how very blessed we are that through the love he "lavished" upon us and our small, childlike faith, itself a gift from God, now we are called children of God. How blessed we are! And it is totally and completely his unmerited gift to us. We have done nothing to deserve our new name nor our favored status. They are ours purely through his marvelous love and grace. How blessed we are that the Father should love us so!

As I think of how blessed we are, I cannot help but think of those children who have never heard of the love of our heavenly Parent. I think of those who have never known the love of an earthly parent or worse, have suffered abuse at the hand of an unloving one. I think of those who live lives of self-destruction which stems largely from never knowing such love. I think of those who walk a painful path living lives warped because they only mimic the hatred and violence in which they have been reared. How blessed are we who have not had to endure such.

On a lighter note, I must confess to something. When I cannot avoid it, when there is no other alternative, when I cannot get out of it, when I am forced to do so, I play with my fifteen-month-old grandson! Talk about God's gift of pure, unadulterated joy! We have our little games we play. Our newest one is where we turn together the handle on our old ring-type wall telephone and I speak into the mouthpiece, "Hello!" And then I hold him up to the mouthpiece and he says, "Huh-uh!" I think he enjoys it almost as much as I do. Then I thought, he is doing exactly what I do! He is saying exactly what I say! That is the most frightening thing in the world to me. Well, almost! The most frightening thing is to observe words and behavior that I instilled long ago in my three sons. I think about all those without God's love who only do and say what they perceive all around them. It makes us feel all the more grateful of our status as children of God, especially when we remember that we have done nothing to deserve it.

It would be hard to imagine anyone receiving more honors and accolades. He was Wisemen of America's number one high school quarterback. He was the Associated Press' number one high school football and basketball player in America, 1961. He signed a college football scholarship to play for the legendary Paul "Bear" Bryant at the University of Alabama, where he was the starting quarterback in three major bowl games. He was chosen All-American, the "Most Valuable Player" in the 1966 Orange Bowl, Atlanta Touchdown Club's Most Valuable Player in the Southeastern Conference, 1965, and winner of the Sammy Baugh Trophy presented by the Columbus, Ohio, Touchdown Club, 1965. These are only a sampling of his many honors. But, Steve Sloan later stated that the greatest honor he ever received was from a less-than-friendly student who pushed him aside while passing him on his college campus and said, "Get out of the way, Christian!" The greatest honor he ever received was to be called Christian — a child of God.

We will never receive a greater honor than to be called Christian nor one that we deserve less! John 1:12-13 says: "Yet to all who received him, to those who believed in his name, he gave the right to become children of God, children born not of natural descent nor of human decision or a husband's will but born of God."

How blessed we are to be named children of God! But often this present reality is called into question by an unbelieving world. "The reason the world does not know us is that it did not know him" (v. 1b). Our status as God's child is sometimes called into question by an unbelieving world. Often our status is called into question because we are different from an unbelieving world that does not understand us, especially as Christians become more and more a minority. The unbelievers scratch their heads and say, "Those folks are different!" They think we dress funny with robes and sashes. Our buildings sometimes intimidate and our language seems "coded." What is it with all these "thee's and thou's" and terms like redemption, reconciliation, and rapture? They watch religious entertainers on television and wonder what this has to do with everyday life. They criticize those who always seem to be begging for money. Our music, mode of dress, and morality are foreign to them, and they remark, "Are these guys weird or what?" We are sometimes perceived as being different.

On the other hand, our status as children of God is sometimes called into question because we are no different from the unbelieving world. They put their thumbs behind their suspenders and remark, "I'm just as good as that Christian. He is no different than I am." They observe our denominational political fusses and say, "They're no different!" They chide us because of fallen leaders and ask, "Are you unique?" Often in our morality we are no different than the unbelieving world around us and give to them the excuse they have been looking for to remain in disbelief. They echo the sentiment of the Nihilistic philosopher Frederick Nietzsche, "If you want me to believe in your Redeemer, you first have to show me that you have been redeemed." They say, "You are no different at all!" And, too often, they are right! Yes, Virginia, there are hypocrites in the church! But I cannot think of a better place for a hypocrite to be than in the church. Better to be a hypocrite in the church than out!

Don Harbuck quoted an old George W. Truett story. It seemed that a man once came to Dr. Truett and demanded that his name be removed from the church roll. He did not want to be a Christian any more. Truett responded, "I will, but I am behind in my work now. If you will visit Mrs. So-and-So who just lost her husband, read some scripture, and have prayer with her, I will honor the request." The man refused. "Okay, but that's the only way I can do what you ask since I am so far behind." The man reluctantly agreed. He visited the widow, read scripture, and prayed with her and never again asked to have his name removed. His Christian action reminded him of his nature bestowed upon him by God's grace. He could not deny who he was. He was a child of God.

Because of the Father's love we are the children of God whether we are perceived to be by an unbelieving world or not. John continues by saying that we also are becoming what we are. "Dear friends, now we are children of God, and what we will be has not yet been made known. But we know that when he appears, we shall be like him, for we shall see him as he is" (v. 2). We are children of God and we are becoming children of God. There is to our status a "now and not yet." We inherit eternal life now which is completed when we die or Christ comes again. We share Christ's life today as we become more and more like him, a process to be completed in heaven. The fancy theological term is "realized eschatology" made prominent by the great theologian, C. H. Dodd.

We are a child and are becoming a child. But to become more of what we are, we must make a response. The dynamic is similar to the experience of the younger son in Jesus' greatest story, sometimes called the parable of the Loving Father. After wasting his inheritance, the son found himself destitute in the mire of the pigpen. He was still a "son," but he initiated the process of becoming what he was when he "came to himself" and started the journey back to the Father. And, of course, the prodigal's Father received him joyfully as a full "son" in the Father's house. We are and we are becoming.

I saw a sign in the hospital which read, "God loves me just the way I am and too much to let me stay that way." Possibly that means that every child of God is an unfinished product. Perhaps it means that God "ain't through with us yet." Perhaps it means that God is still at work in our lives. There is a legend which has an individual asking the great artist Michelangelo, "How are you able to take a simple, formless block of stone and from it produce a beautiful angel?" The sculptor replied, "It is simple. I just chisel away everything that does not look like an angel." Perhaps this means that every day God sculpts, chisels, and chips away everything in us that does not look like Jesus. God still is at work to make us distinctively different.

But we have work to do as well. The process of becoming more and more like Christ demands our response. "We know we shall be like him ... Everyone who has this hope in him purifies himself, just as he is pure" (vv. 2b-3). We must cooperate with God as he molds us into the image of his Son (Romans 8:29). I am not sure that I know what John means by "purify," but maybe it is similar to an experience I had as a young man. For three summers I worked at the Republic Steel Mill to earn money for college. Nine thousand employees worked there, and they were supervised by 550 foremen, one of whom was my father. Of those 550 foremen, my father was ranked number two in their work-simplification rating system. Everyone knew him. The first week I was there, the labor foreman painted "CARVER" across my hard hat which I wore at all times. Countless persons would see my hat and remark, "So, you're Carver's kid!" Then, they would watch. They watched to see how hard I worked, how well I listened, how fast I learned. They watched to see if I lived up to my name. We all have work to do to live up to our name Christian — "Little Christ." We are in process of becoming what we are — a process that will continue throughout all eternity.

I was privileged to study in seminary under the great preacher and Old Testament scholar, Clyde Francisco. Dr. Francisco used to say, "Oh, we will continue to grow in heaven because we will continue to have problems. The only difference between heaven and here is that there will be some answers in heaven. There are no answers to the problems we face here!" How true! How blessed we are to be able to look forward to an eternity in which to grow in Christ-likeness.

You may have heard the story going around of two caterpillars crawling around in the grit, grass, and dirt of the ground. Overhead was flying gracefully a beautiful multi-colored butterfly. Looking up, one caterpillar said to the other, "I know one thing. You'll never get me up there in one of those contraptions!" There is just no telling what God is going to do in our lives — in this world and the next.

As Soren Kierkegaard, the Danish philosopher, said, "The root of sin is the refusal to be what God has created us to be." Why don't we let God do all he wants to do with us?

If ever I knew a child of God it was she. Over fifty women filed into her Bible study class each Sunday. She stood at the door and hugged each one. She had forgotten more Bible than I have ever known. She knew the literary classics and could quote poetry endlessly without flaw. She had given herself tirelessly to multiple mission projects. She was a saint.

She lived alone and very modestly, her husband and son long deceased. When she died, she did not own an automobile. Yet, she gave annually to our church budget an amount near $125,000. She once gave $100,000 to the scholarship fund at the seminary from which I graduated because I remarked once in a sermon that I could not have made it through seminary without scholarships. During the pledging portion for a recent building campaign, she approached me to say that she was going to give her Coca-Cola stock at that time because she "did not want me to get in trouble over the building campaign." Over 33,000 shares netted over $1,750,000. She literally saved my pastorate. When she died, she left to the church the rest of her estate which totaled another $1,500,000. I was her pastor. She was my "Rufus mother" (Romans 16:13). I loved Bess Hill.

She was so alive and vibrant, it was easy to forget that she was almost ninety and very nearly blind. On Sunday morning she greeted and hugged everyone as usual. On Tuesday morning, she fell. I saw her in the hospital around noon and she seemed to be fine. I returned around 4:00 p.m. and her condition had markedly changed. "Oh, hello, darling," she said as she always did. But I knew she was much worse. After a few moments, I asked, "Bess, are you all right?" She looked at me with a gaze still embedded in my mind. "No," she said, "but I will be soon." She knew. Six hours later, I held her hand as she went on to be with her Lord — as she went on to become more and more of what she so beautifully was.

**Thanksgiving
2 Corinthians 9:6-15**

Describing The Indescribable

"Thanks be to God for his indescribable gift!" (v. 15).

How do you describe something that is indescribable? Have you ever tried to describe something which cannot be described?

In 1666 the great fire of London destroyed much of the city. Christopher Wren was chosen to serve as the major architect to rebuild the city from the rubbish. His greatest challenge was to be the architect for the rebuilding of St. Paul's Cathedral, a task at which he spent 35 years of his life. When the project was completed, the reigning monarch of the day, Queen Ann, was given a guided tour of the edifice by Christopher Wren. When she viewed the structure upon which he had given the major effort of his life's work, her remarks were, "It is awful; it is artificial; it is amusing."

Now, what if someone had made those comments about a work upon which you had spent 35 years? You and I might be devastated. Christopher Wren gave a huge sight of relief, said, "Thank you, your Majesty," and bowed at her feet. Why? Because in seventeenth century England, those words had different meanings than they have today. In those days "awful" meant "awe-inspiring," "artificial" meant "artistic," and "amusing" meant "amazing."[1] No wonder Wren was pleased. Queen Ann was giving to him the highest compliment of his time. And there are those who have seen it who say that even her words did not do justice to the work of Sir Christopher Wren.

How does one describe that which cannot be described? Paul states that God's gift to us is indescribable. The word in the original language means "inexpressible," "unutterable" or "cannot be related." It literally is a gift beyond description.

Why is it that sometimes a thing is inexpressible or unutterable? It could be that we find it so difficult, if not impossible, to describe something because we lack the language, especially when words vary so in their connotation, as seen with Queen Ann's reaction. Take the word "bad." When I grew up the word "bad" meant "bad." When you called someone "bad" it meant that they were bad or unethical or not good. Today, "bad" does not mean "bad." Today "bad" means "good." If you say to someone, "Hey, that's a bad sweater!" that means that it is a good sweater or a stylish one. So, "bad" means "good" or "stylish."

Last week I was in a car rental office and the clerk was having a very difficult time checking in my car. He could not get the computer to print out my statement. Finally, another worker came over and said, "Man, you've got to click on it!" To which my clerk said, "Oh, no, I see! My 'bad.'"

Now, wait a minute! Did he mean that he was "bad" or "good" or "stylish"? No, he meant that he had made a mistake. So, bad can mean "bad" or "good" or "stylish" or "a mistake." I am confused! And, I am not even going to try to explain the title of Michael Jackson's musical album which is titled, you guessed it, "BAD!"

So, it is difficult to describe something because of the changing nature and context of language. Also, it can be a challenge to express something because it is so far beyond us or is even mysterious. I understand that Albert Einstein's Theory of Relativity can be expressed by the formula $e=mc^2$? I think that I remember that "e" stands for energy, "m" stands for mass and somehow "c" expressed the velocity of light squared. While I have a hint of the meaning of the various compounds, I am a great distance away from being able to describe the theory. It is a mystery beyond this very finite mind to understand or my limited language to describe.

Often something is impossible to describe because it is beyond words. How do you describe the Grand Canyon? "Well, there's some rocks, mountains, a little river, and vegetation. Oh, yes, there are many bright colors!" If you have ever stood on the rim of the

Grand Canyon and beheld its splendor, you might say that my description falls woefully short. Or, how would you describe the face of a six-month-old baby? "Well, she has a cute button nose and huge brown eyes, her hair is swirled up into a pink ribbon, and she has cute chubby cheeks." Does that do it? Hardly! You have to see her or kiss those chubby cheeks! How does one explain the taste of vanilla ice cream to one who has never tasted ice cream, or creme brulee, or an Almond Joy, which is supposed to be "indescribably delicious?" You can't! The person must experience it! Some things are indescribable! They must be experienced in a firsthand, personal way!

In our text, Paul states that we can experience firsthand one of God's most essential characteristics if not the very essence of his nature. That is the characteristic of "generosity." God is generous! We can be generous as well, especially as we participate in his indescribable gift.

We begin to experience God's generosity when we realize and remember that God is a giver. "As it is written: He has scattered abroad his gifts to the poor; his righteousness endures forever" (v. 9). His gift of generosity begins to be ours when we realize that everything we have had, have, or ever hope to have or be are gracious gifts of God's bountiful, generous nature. We remember that these are gifts to be cherished and appreciated but never to be hoarded selfishly.

In the movie *Wall Street*, the Michael Douglas character tries to persuade a group of stockholders that his intended takeover is good, not bad, because "Greed is Good." He states that greed is so good it shall be the salvation of our troubled society. While few would express it so bluntly, there are those, legion in number, who live to acquire, amass, and accumulate. Tragically, too often, the world's economy states, "He who has the most toys wins!"

Paradoxically, God's economy states just the opposite!

> *And God is able to make all grace abound to you, so that in all things at all times, having all that you need, you will abound in every good work ... Now he who supplies seed to the sower and bread for food will also*

> *supply and increase your store of seed and will enlarge the harvest of your righteousness. You will be made rich in every way so that you can be generous on every occasion, and through us your generosity will result in thanksgiving to God.*
> — 2 Corinthians 9:8, 10-11

Paul says that we can share in God's economy. He states that God generously supplies our needs in order that we can generously supply the needs of others. The more generous we are, the more generous we become. The more generous we become, the more thankful we are. The more thankful we are, the more joyful we are and the more glory God receives! God's economy is this ever-spiraling and expanding effect of generosity, gratitude, and joyfulness, which produces more generosity, gratitude, and joy.

It is also good theology. God's economy also produces the right kind of generous faith that is free to give today because it trusts God's provision for tomorrow.

It is similar to the experience of the widow at Zarephath (1 Kings 17:7-24) who gave to the prophet Elijah all that she had only to find that our generous God supplied her needs in a never ending supply.

It is similar to the statement of English poet Rudyard Kipling to the graduating class of McGill University when he challenged them not to focus upon or care for money, power, or fame. "Someday you will meet someone who cares for none of these things ... then you will realize how poor you are."

It is similar to the statement of Saint Augustine, who once defined sin as "using what one ought to enjoy and enjoying what one ought to use."[2] John Claypool here explains that Augustine is talking about the ends and means of life. To "use" has to do with means. I can "use" something beyond that for which it was intended. For example, "I used him to get the promotion I desired." To "enjoy" has to do with ends. To enjoy means to appreciate something for what it is and nothing more. I can enjoy God and give to him the glory that is his due.

In man's earliest efforts at religion, he sought to "buy off" God through gifts and sacrifice. He felt that if his sacrifices were big enough, his works of righteousness piled high enough, God would certainly be in his debt and he could "use" God to fulfill his selfish desires. I could hardly believe it when a church leader once said to me, "If I do such and such, then God has to do what I say!" Again while few of us would seek to express it so bluntly, we often operate under the assumption that God will reward our faithfulness with our idea of success, not necessarily his!

God's economy paradoxically promotes just the opposite. Generously, gratefully, joyfully, we give to God because he is generous, gracious, and joyful. We share in his nature and share in his glory. We don't seek to "use" God, we seek to enjoy him. We seek to share in the characteristic of his generosity as we become more and more like him. We seek to become distinctively different as he is "holy other" — distinctively different. As states the Westminster catechism, "The chief end of man is to love God and to enjoy him forever."

Perhaps we would do well to recall why Paul was writing this letter to the church at Corinth in the first place. Paul was encouraging the Gentile Christians at the church in Corinth to support the relief offering for the Jewish Christians at the church in Jerusalem. A rift had occurred! The division between Jewish and Gentile Christianity was widening. Paul felt that a genuine display of generosity on the part of Gentile Christianity would go a long way in helping to heal the growing separation. Paul was right. Nothing brings people together so much as a display of love and generosity. Defenses are melted. Offenses are forgotten. Camaraderie is recognized. It's somewhat like when different Christians gather around one table in gratitude for the generosity of God in sending his only Son to die for us undeserving sinners.

In a Sunday evening Chapel Eucharist Service two Christians were taking communion. One was James Mills, who is developmentally challenged. Another was Christine Boyd, who is blind. James escorted Christine into the service, guided her through the liturgy, and held the elements for her and assisted her as we recognized our common Savior. Two people, though different, were one — whole in God's generous, indescribable gift.

Several years ago a layman by the name of Steve Tondera led our Deacon's Retreat. Shortly after the retreat, he went to his high school reunion in Texas. Steve grew up in Waco. In high school, he hung around with five other boys who hung around six other girls. Just buddies. It was just natural that when the group divided up it seemed that Steve was always with Ina Blayne. Ina Blayne was not very pretty, a little overweight, and the daughter of blue-collar parents. They didn't have a lot, but life was good.

As the class members were congregating and talking at the reunion, there was almost a hush in the crowd as a beautiful lady walked in with diamonds and furs everywhere. Steve asked J. B. Hensley, one of his old high school buddies, "Wow, who is that?" He said, "Don't you know? That's Ina Blayne." "That's Ina Blayne?" "She's filthy rich."

Steve walked over, gave her a big hug and they began to get reacquainted. He said, "You look wonderful! Wow, what has happened to you?" She said, "You see that limousine out there and the chauffeur? That's mine. Everything my husband Harlan touches turns to money."

Then Steve said, "I don't know why I said it, but I just said, 'Ina Blayne, why don't you use some of your money to help others?'" She said, "What?" "Why don't you give some of your money away to people who are in need?" She said, "What do you mean?" "You could give it to a school or something. Why don't you give it to Baylor University right here in Waco?" She said, "I never went to college, much less Baylor." He said, "That doesn't matter. There's people at Baylor who could use some of that money." She said, "Oh, you're kidding. How would I do something like that?" He said, "Call up the president, Dr. Reynolds, and I promise you he'll meet with you if you tell him you want to give him some money." She asked, "Are you sure about this?" Steve replied, "Believe me, he will meet with you!" He continued, "You remember when we were in high school and you wanted to go to church camp but lacked the funds. You remember that our pastor, Brother Sutherland, gave you the six dollars to go?" She said, "You know, I do remember that." Steve said, "You could do the same with your money."

"I'll think about that!" she said. Steve said that the whole conversation lasted less than ten minutes.

About eight weeks later Steve received a call from Ina Blayne. "Steve, we did it!" "Did what?" "We met with Dr. Reynolds and endowed a chair at Baylor University in the School of Religion." He said, "You're kidding." "No, I'm not kidding at all." "That's wonderful and I know that your husband is honored to have a chair endowed in his name." He said, "I've just got to ask you, how much did you give?" She said, "Well, you know Brother Sutherland gave me six dollars and I graduated in 1952 so my husband and I gave to Baylor University $652,000, but I did not endow that chair in the name of my husband. I endowed it in the name of Brother Sutherland."

You see the cycle, don't you? The ever-expanding cycle of God's economy? It goes from generosity to gratitude to joy to generosity to ...

Let me ask you, who was generous? Was it Steve who listened to God's Spirit to give less than ten minutes of his time? Was it Harlan who worked to earn and complied with his wife's wishes? Was it Ina Blayne who converted past generosity into a present and never-ending one? Was it Brother Sutherland who gave six dollars not knowing that God would expand it far beyond his wildest imagination? Was it God who was generous as he always is in an effort to help us experience his heavenly economy? And the answer would be, "Yes!"

---

1. John R. Claypool, "God is an Amateur," an unpublished sermon preached at the Northminster Baptist Church, Jackson, Mississippi, September 2, 1979.

2. John R. Claypool, "A Cheerful Giver," an unpublished sermon preached at the Crescent Hill Baptist Church, Louisville, Kentucky, October 15, 1967.

**Christ The King
Ephesians 1:15-23**

A Prayer For Maturing Faith

I make no secret of the fact that I am not fond of bumper stickers or bumper sticker religion. However, I did see one the other day that caused a smile and a nod of agreement. It read, "Be patient! God is not finished with me yet!" I like that! It reminds me that I am still very much a work in process and, I hope, in progress. With apologies to Robert Fulgham, I did not learn everything I need to know in kindergarten. Where I was reared, we did not even have a kindergarten, so, needless to say it is difficult to learn from that which one never attended. But my educational process, though deprived early on, continues today. It also is true to say that the more I learn, the more I realize how much there is to learn and how little I know.

I think the dynamic also is true in the realm of spiritual matters. The more I learn about Jesus and the closer to him I become, the more I realize how much more there is of Christ to know and how woefully short I fall in comparison to his marvelous example. I still have a way to go. However, I find encouragement in our text because it reminds me that Paul, the Apostle, is praying for me.

Let me try to explain. The New Testament book of Ephesians, more perhaps than any other of Paul's letters, is a circular letter. In fact, the word "Ephesians" does not appear at the beginning of many of our older and better manuscripts. That could mean that "Ephesians" is a summary of Paul's theology to a group of churches that was to be circulated from one church to another. Therefore, a circular letter. Perhaps, this letter is not just for one congregation at Ephesus where Paul spent three years, but for all congregations. The letter is not so much for one time as it is for all times. Therefore, when Paul writes in verse 16, "I have not stopped giving thanks for you, remembering you in my prayers," he is not only praying for first-century Christians, he is also praying for twentieth- and twenty-first-century Christians. Just think, Paul is praying for you and me.

What an encouragement to think that Paul is praying for us! He is praying that we would know Christ better (v. 17) or that we would have a maturing faith. I know few who have a mature faith, but I am acquainted with several whose faith is maturing. Paul is praying that ours would be a faith that is alive, expanding, bringing us closer to God and making us distinctively different in the image of his Son Jesus.

Paul uses two beautiful word pictures to paint a description of this ever-maturing faith. The first metaphor used to explain this faith is the word "wisdom." In Paul's usage, wisdom means more than just knowledge or information. Wisdom is more akin to spiritual discernment coupled with the ability to apply knowledge in practical and spiritual ways. In scripture, wisdom is a gift of God.

The second, very similar to wisdom, is the word picture "revelation," which also is a gift of the Holy Spirit. In the Bible, the Holy Spirit has at least two functions. First, the Holy Spirit is to reveal or disclose God and his truth to us. Secondly, the Holy Spirit gives to us the ability to recognize and discern that truth when we see it and apply his truth according to his will. Thus, this revelation and wisdom is given to us that "we may know him better" (v. 17). Paul then proceeds to pray that the "eyes of our heart might be enlightened" (v. 18). What a beautiful phrase — "the eyes of our heart." Paul is praying that we may have eyes of discernment to see things as God sees them.

The eyes of the heart! One might see a newborn baby as messy and wrinkled, while another sees the most miraculous event in the world. The eyes of the heart! One might see a street person dirty and deserving of his plight in life, while another may see a person for whom Christ died and an opportunity to put our religious talk into action. The eyes of the heart! Could it be that Paul is praying that, in some small way, we might see as God does? That is a maturing faith. That is a life that is distinctively different.

In our text, Paul describes the Christian whose faith is maturing. Maturing Christians are ones who know where they are going, whose they are, and who have the means to arrive at their destination.

The maturing Christian knows where he or she is going. Paul states, "I pray that your eyes may be enlightened in order that you may know the hope to which he has called you, the riches of his glorious inheritance of the saints" (v. 18). That "hope and inheritance" is nothing less than a call to share in the very life of Christ. Every one of us is called to be distinctively different, as was Jesus. As Fred Craddock states, "If there was a governing metaphor in the message of Jesus, it very well may be that the very life and presence of Christ can be yours!" Jesus' very life can be ours? We can be as joyful, kind, graceful, forgiving, compassionate, and loving as Jesus? That is quite a hope! That is quite an inheritance!

Let me ask you: Are you closer to Jesus today than you were last year? Are you more like Jesus today than you were this time last year? Are you more loving? Are you kinder? Are you more forgiving? Are you reflecting more and more the nature and spirit of Jesus? Are you any more like Jesus than you were ten years ago, five years ago? Are you still struggling with the same problems that you were struggling with ten years ago, fifteen years ago, five years ago? Does God want it to be that way? God has called you that you may realize the hope of being more like Jesus.

Mother Teresa says that the first step toward a maturing faith is to will it. The first step is to have a determination to do so. Have you made that determination?

Mohammed Ali was a three-time world heavyweight boxing champion. His face has appeared on the cover of *Sports Illustrated* more times than any other athlete. Some have tabbed him as the greatest athlete of the twentieth century. He has one of the most recognizable faces of anyone in the world. When he was "floating like a butterfly and stinging like a bee," he was king of the sports world. His entourage followed him around the globe. But where is he now? Gary Smith, a reporter, went to see Ali. Ali escorted him out to a barn next to his farmhouse. On the floor, leaning against the walls, were mementos of Ali in his hey day. Photos were endless of his sculpted body, at its prime performing seemingly the impossible — the knockout of George Foreman — the "thrilla in Manilla."

On the photos were white streaks — bird droppings. For some reason Ali walked over to the photos and turned them one by one toward the wall. Then he walked to the barn door, stared at the countryside, and mumbled something. The reporter did not hear what he was saying and he asked him to repeat it. Ali said, "I had the world, and it wasn't nothin'. Look now."[1]

The Roman emperor Charlemagne left very specific instructions for his burial. He wanted to be buried sitting on his throne, scepter in hand, crown on his head, royal cape around his shoulders, and an open book in his lap. He died in 1814 A.D. Two hundred years later Emperor Othello wanted to check to see that Charlemagne's instructions were carried out. They allegedly sent a group of men to exhume him and sure enough, the instructions he left were carried out exactly as he wished. The open book was on his lap with his finger pointed to the place where he requested, Matthew 16:26, which reads, "What does it profit a man if he gains the whole world and loses his soul?"[2]

Maturing Christians are ones who have their priorities right. They are living lives to be more like Jesus of Nazareth. They are living more and more in the nature and spirit and love of Jesus Christ. They know where they are going. They know the hope to which they are called.

Maturing Christians not only know where they are going, they know whose or who they are. They are called to be "saints." The word "saint" in the New Testament is built upon a little Greek root word which means "separate." The word "holy" is built upon this same root word. The Christian is to be "holy" or "separate" in the same way that God is "holy" or "separate." We are to be different as God is different because we are his children. We are heirs of God and joint heirs of Christ (Romans 8:16-17). What a glorious inheritance!

But we sometimes have spiritual amnesia. We forget who we are. We forget that God has created us in his image. We forget that we are one for whom Christ died. As a result, we get caught up in the mad dash of the world in the game of one-upmanship.

Every now and then I like to watch a television show about nothing. Of course, you know that the show is *Seinfeld*. It literally is about nothing. But every so often they slip in a thought worth noting. In a recent episode, Seinfeld discovered that he was number four on someone's speed dial. He became obsessed with the notion that he had to be number one. He spent the entire episode bringing flowers, gifts, doing favors, all in an effort to cause the person to list him number one on the speed dial. How silly! How ridiculous! But when we look at some of the recognition for which we strive, Seinfeld does not seem so foolish. Or does he?

Maturing Christians know who or whose they are. We are created in the image of God. Look at the person to your right or left. That is the very image of God. That is the very best that God can do! That is, you are, God's "masterpiece."

Mother Teresa states that "if you are humble, nothing will touch you, neither praise nor disgrace, because you know what you are ... Christ tells us to aim very high, not to be like Abraham or David or any of the saints, but to be like our heavenly Father."[3]

Do you know whose you are today? Do you know the glorious inheritance that is yours because you are his child? Is your faith maturing? Are you growing more and more like the one you hope to emulate, Jesus Christ our Lord?

A young girl asked her Sunday school teacher, "If Jesus is on the right hand of God, where are we?" The teacher in a moment of insight said, "We're on the other side. We're on the left."[4] Just think: Everything Jesus has in heaven one day shall be yours. You are an heir of God, you are a joint heir of Jesus Christ. And it is God's purpose for you to share in his very life that you might become more and more like him.

Paul's prayer for us is that we might know where we are going, whose we are, and have the resources with which to arrive at our destination. "And his incomparably great power for us who believe. That power is like the working of his mighty strength which he exerted in Christ when he raised him from the dead and seated him at his right hand in the heavenly realms" (vv. 19-20). We travel our road toward maturity in Christ not in our own power but his — not through our own efforts but in his grace. When we travel in his power, we are assured of his success.

We can walk each and every day unafraid with Jesus Christ at our side because God "has placed all things under his feet ..." (v. 22). Look again at the great doxology of praise in verses 22-23: "And God placed all things under his feet and appointed him to be head over everything for the church which is his body, the fulness of him who fills everything in every way." As Major Ian Thomas states, "Everything that is over you is already under him."

Everything that is over your head is already under his feet. Everything that annoys you, defeats you, tempts you, everything that is over you already is under him. How can we lose? So we go forth in life boldly as his children with a maturing faith, knowing where we are going, knowing whose we are, and knowing how we are going to get there.

Tony Campolo tells the story of his neighbor's four-year-old daughter. He said that if you put her in a Shirley Temple look-a-like contest, she would win every time. One night after her parents put her to bed, there arose a tremendous thunderstorm. The lightning was flashing all around, the thundering was making a loud rolling noise, the wind was blowing the rain against the windows. The father ran upstairs to check on the daughter, "Honey, are you all right?" As he opened the door, she was standing up against the window spread out like an eagle. "Honey, what are you doing?" She turned around with a great big smile on her face and said, "God is trying to take my picture!" Wouldn't that be a wonderful way to go through life? "God is trying to take my picture." No fear! No worry! No dread! No apprehension! Living in the hands of God and interpreting every event through the grace and love of God.

His name is Gordon Gund. Gordon had a fairly normal life until his mid-thirties when he was stricken with an illness that took his eyesight. The illness left him totally blind. He descended into despair. Then he began to call upon the resources of his family and his faith. His attitude was transformed to see things in a positive light. He began to look at what he had and not what he did not have. He began reconstructing his life. His eyes were opened in a real sense. Today Gordon Gund is the owner of the NBA franchise, the Cleveland Cavaliers, and has established a foundation for eye research. His eyes were truly opened to see what was important in life. He not only knew where he was going, he knew who he was.[5]

William Borden was born to power, influence, and prestige. He received the finest education at Yale University. He left all and went to serve God and his fellow man in Egypt. As a result of his untiring service to God and fellow man, he died very young. Written on his tombstone in Cairo, Egypt, you will find these words, "Apart from Christ there is no explanation for such a life."[6]

Is that the life you live? Christ is the explanation for where we are going, who we are, and how we're going to get there. Christ is the essence of life. He is the center of our thoughts! He is the direction of our love! He is the object of our worship! He is the Lord of our life! What a prayer! Thank you, Paul, for praying for us.

Dr. Joel Avery is a thoracic surgeon and a deacon at the church where I serve as pastor. While touring the exhibit hall at the National Convention of the Cooperative Baptist Fellowship in Birmingham he was approached by a missionary who has to remain unidentified for security reasons. Many "unofficial" missionaries of the Cooperative Baptist Fellowship have to remain anonymous because the country in which they serve does not allow "official" missionaries. The nameless missionary approached Joel. Reading Dr. Avery's name tag, he began, "You are a member at First Baptist in Chattanooga, right? I have been looking for someone from your church for years to tell this story." And with that he unfolded a most incredible episode to Dr. Avery.

"You remember that my wife and I spoke at your church at the beginning of the Gulf War? We requested that you pray for us as I was leaving your church to go straight to the airport in Atlanta to return to Turkey. I still had members of my 'missionary team' trapped in Iraq and I was returning to get them out. When I arrived in Iraq near the Turkish border, I encountered a United States Army colonel who stated that the situation was very dangerous due to Saddam Hussein's activities. I asked the colonel if he would send in a team to retrieve my people, and he said that would be impossible. I stated then that I would go myself, and he adamantly refused to allow me to go. 'How am I going to get my people out?' I asked. 'I don't know, but no one is going in there.' 'What am I to do?' I asked. 'Call the President or something! It is out of my hands,' the colonel responded. 'That's exactly what I'll do!' I replied."

With that the missionary returned to his less-than-luxurious hotel and, to his great surprise, found the only telephone on his hotel floor unoccupied. That in itself was a minor miracle. Where to call? The only telephone number he had was that of the hotel in Houston where his wife was speaking at a mission's conference at the Tallowwood Baptist Church. To his amazement she answered the phone. She had had to return to the hotel room because of trouble with her contact lens. He quickly related his predicament and said, "You have to call the President." "Which President?" "Of the United States!" he cried.

"Well, I just can't pick up the phone and call the President, but Keith Parks is at the church. I'll see if he can help." Keith Parks was the Director of International Missions for the Cooperative Baptist Fellowship. After being told the story, Parks said, "All I know to do is to call James Dunn, Executive Director of the Baptist Joint Committee in Washington, D.C." Parks then called James Dunn at 5:00 p.m. and to his surprise found Dunn at home. Dunn is never at home at 5:00 p.m. Having been caught just out of the shower and after hearing the story, Dunn told Parks, "Well, Keith, if you'll quit talking, I'm trying to get dressed to go to a dinner at the White House. Let's see what we can do."

When James Dunn entered the White House dinner, he was immediately approached by Hillary Clinton to thank him for some favorable comments he recently had made about her to the press. Dunn quickly related the predicament of the nameless missionary. Hillary responded, "I will help if I can. Let's go talk to Bill."

About midnight, the missionary received a knock upon his hotel door. When he answered he saw a slightly embarrassed United

States Army colonel. He stuttered, "I have just sent in a team to get your people out. And, yes, please don't ever call the President of the United States on me again!"

The incredible entire process of one miracle after another occurred in a time period of less than six hours!

"I just wanted to thank someone from First Baptist Church of Chattanooga for praying for us. Next time I need a miracle I am going to ask you all to pray. You folks know how to get results!" So does Paul! Aren't you glad that he is praying for you?

---

1. Max Lucado, *The Applause Of Heaven* (Dallas: Word Publishing, 1990), p. 152.

2. *Ibid.,* p. 153.

3. Mother Teresa, *No Greater Love* (Novato, California: New World Library, 1997), p. 55.

4. Mark J. Molldrem, *The Victory Of Faith* (Lima, Ohio: CSS Publishing Company, 1997), p. 81.

5. Molldrem, *op. cit.,* p. 29.

6. *Preaching,* Volume VIII, Number 5, March-April, 1993 (Jacksonville: Preaching Resources, Inc.), p. 68.

Lectionary Preaching After Pentecost

The following index will aid the user of this book in matching the correct Sunday with the appropriate text during Pentecost. All texts in this book are from the series for the Second Reading, Revised Common Lectionary. (Note that the ELCA division of Lutheranism is now following the Revised Common Lectionary.) The Lutheran designations indicate days comparable to Sundays on which Revised Common Lectionary Propers or Ordinary Time designations are used.

(Fixed dates do not pertain to Lutheran Lectionary)

Fixed Date Lectionaries *Revised Common (including ELCA)* *and Roman Catholic*	Lutheran Lectionary *Lutheran*
The Day of Pentecost	The Day of Pentecost
The Holy Trinity	The Holy Trinity
May 29-June 4 — Proper 4, Ordinary Time 9	Pentecost 2
June 5-11 — Proper 5, Ordinary Time 10	Pentecost 3
June 12-18 — Proper 6, Ordinary Time 11	Pentecost 4
June 19-25 — Proper 7, Ordinary Time 12	Pentecost 5
June 26-July 2 — Proper 8, Ordinary Time 13	Pentecost 6
July 3-9 — Proper 9, Ordinary Time 14	Pentecost 7
July 10-16 — Proper 10, Ordinary Time 15	Pentecost 8
July 17-23 — Proper 11, Ordinary Time 16	Pentecost 9
July 24-30 — Proper 12, Ordinary Time 17	Pentecost 10
July 31-Aug. 6 — Proper 13, Ordinary Time 18	Pentecost 11
Aug. 7-13 — Proper 14, Ordinary Time 19	Pentecost 12
Aug. 14-20 — Proper 15, Ordinary Time 20	Pentecost 13
Aug. 21-27 — Proper 16, Ordinary Time 21	Pentecost 14
Aug. 28-Sept. 3 — Proper 17, Ordinary Time 22	Pentecost 15
Sept. 4-10 — Proper 18, Ordinary Time 23	Pentecost 16
Sept. 11-17 — Proper 19, Ordinary Time 24	Pentecost 17
Sept. 18-24 — Proper 20, Ordinary Time 25	Pentecost 18

Sept. 25-Oct. 1 — Proper 21, Ordinary Time 26	Pentecost 19
Oct. 2-8 — Proper 22, Ordinary Time 27	Pentecost 20
Oct. 9-15 — Proper 23, Ordinary Time 28	Pentecost 21
Oct. 16-22 — Proper 24, Ordinary Time 29	Pentecost 22
Oct. 23-29 — Proper 25, Ordinary Time 30	Pentecost 23
Oct. 30-Nov. 5 — Proper 26, Ordinary Time 31	Pentecost 24
Nov. 6-12 — Proper 27, Ordinary Time 32	Pentecost 25
Nov. 13-19 — Proper 28, Ordinary Time 33	Pentecost 26
	Pentecost 27
Nov. 20-26 — Christ the King	Christ the King

Reformation Day (or last Sunday in October) is October 31 (Revised Common, Lutheran)

All Saints' Day (or first Sunday in November) is November 1 (Revised Common, Lutheran, Roman Catholic)

Books In This Cycle A Series

GOSPEL SET
It's News To Me! Messages Of Hope For Those Who Haven't Heard
Sermons For Advent/Christmas/Epiphany
Linda Schiphorst McCoy

Tears Of Sadness, Tears Of Gladness
Sermons For Lent/Easter
Albert G. Butzer, III

Pentecost Fire: Preaching Community In Seasons Of Change
Sermons For Sundays After Pentecost (First Third)
Schuyler Rhodes

Questions Of Faith
Sermons For Sundays After Pentecost (Middle Third)
Marilyn Saure Breckenridge

The Home Stretch: Matthew's Vision Of Servanthood In The End-Time
Sermons For Sundays After Pentecost (Last Third)
Mary Sue Dehmlow Dreier

FIRST LESSON SET
Long Time Coming!
Sermons For Advent/Christmas/Epiphany
Stephen M. Crotts

Restoring The Future
Sermons For Lent/Easter
Robert J. Elder

Formed By A Dream
Sermons For Sundays After Pentecost (First Third)
Kristin Borsgard Wee

Living On One Day's Rations
Sermons For Sundays After Pentecost (Middle Third)
Douglas B. Bailey

Let's Get Committed
Sermons For Sundays After Pentecost (Last Third)
Derl G. Keefer

SECOND LESSON SET
Holy E-Mail
Sermons For Advent/Christmas/Epiphany
Dallas A. Brauninger

Access To High Hope
Sermons For Lent/Easter
Harry N. Huxhold

Acting On The Absurd
Sermons For Sundays After Pentecost (First Third)
Gary L. Carver

A Call To Love
Sermons For Sundays After Pentecost (Middle Third)
Tom M. Garrison

Distinctively Different
Sermons For Sundays After Pentecost (Last Third)
Gary L. Carver